LIBRARY PROGRAMMING

for AUTISTIC CHILDREN *and* TEENS

D1319031

ALA Editions purchases fund advocacy, awareness, and accreditation programs for library professionals worldwide.

LIBRARY PROGRAMMING
for AUTISTIC CHILDREN and TEENS

SECOND EDITION

Amelia Anderson

Foreword by Barbara Klipper

ALA
Editions

CHICAGO 2021

AMELIA ANDERSON, PHD, is an assistant professor of library and information studies at Old Dominion University who has extensive experience on the topic of autism and libraries through her work as a public librarian, library researcher, and educator. She has worked to develop training for librarians to better understand and serve their users on the autism spectrum through two IMLS-funded initiatives, Project PALS and Project A +. Through original research and partnerships with autism self-advocates, Anderson studies and shares best practices and trends at the intersection of autism and libraries, and has presented her work at conferences ranging from local to international audiences.

ISBNs
978-0-8389-9485-6 (paper)
978-0-8389-3805-8 (PDF)

Library of Congress Cataloging-in-Publication Data

Names: Anderson, Amelia, 1983- author. | Klipper, Barbara. Programming for children and teens with autism spectrum disorder.

Title: Library programming for autistic children and teens / Amelia Anderson ; foreword by Barbara Klipper.

Description: Second edition. | Chicago : ALA Editions, 2021. | Includes bibliographical references and index. | Summary: "This edition reflects the new knowledge that has been learned about autism since the publication of the first edition, amplifies the voices of autistic self-advocates, and provides new, easy-to-replicate programming ideas for successfully serving autistic children and teens"—Provided by publisher.

Identifiers: LCCN 2020053383 | ISBN 9780838994856 (paperback) | ISBN 9780838938058 (pdf)

Subjects: LCSH: Libraries and the developmentally disabled. | Autism spectrum disorders in children. | Libraries and teenagers with disabilities. | Children with autism spectrum disorders—Services for. | Youth with autism spectrum disorders—Services for.

Classification: LCC Z711.92.D48 A53 2021 | DDC 027.6/63—dc23

LC record available at https://lccn.loc.gov/2020053383

Cover design by Alejandra Diaz. Book design by Kim Thornton in the Charis and Karbid Slab typefaces.

⊗ This paper meets the requirements of ANSI/NISO Z39.48-1992 (Permanence of Paper).

Printed in the United States of America

25 24 23 22 21   5 4 3 2 1

Contents

Foreword

by Barbara Klipper

I N 2011, NOT LONG AFTER STARTING A GRANT-FUNDED SENSORY STORY-time at the Ferguson Library in Stamford, Connecticut, I organized and presented at a session called "Sensory Storytime: Preschool Programming That Makes Sense for Children with Autism" at that year's ALA Annual Conference. At the time, this type of program was almost unheard-of, and my goal was to bring it to the attention of youth services librarians around the country.

The session was well-attended and appeared to be well-received, and I was relieved when it was over. Then the unbelievable happened. A woman walked up to me brandishing a business card. She asked if I had ever thought about writing a book on the subject. I was floored. I had published a number of articles but never thought of writing a book, but she had planted a seed. Soon after, I developed and submitted a proposal to ALA Editions, which led to my 2014 book, *Programming for Children and Teens with Autism Spectrum Disorder*.

The book got good reviews, including a star in *School Library Journal*, and after its publication I gave conference presentations, webinars, and library system trainings. I became involved with Targeting Autism, an initiative of the Illinois State Library, and I have been presenting at its national forums and serving on its advisory board. I started a grant called "Autism Welcome Here: Library Programs, Services and More," which awards $5,000 in total annually to initiatives that make libraries more accessible to autistic people. The grant committee I put together consisted of me, another youth services librarian, a library director, the creator of Targeting Autism, the director of an autism agency, and an autistic self-advocate. All of these were people I met through Targeting Autism.

Over the five-year history of the grant to date, I have seen a marked change in the sophistication and creativity of the applications. The incidence of autism has increased over that period of time, but so has the response of the library world, and especially youth services, to it.

During this same period, equity, diversity, and inclusion (EDI) in both libraries and its own organization became a goal of the American Library Association.

This goal was championed by Loida Garcia-Febo during her ALA presidency, and it came to the fore as librarians educated themselves about systemic racism, and the Black Lives Matter movement spread across the country. While EDI is most often associated with racial injustice and underrepresentation, it applies equally to people with disabilities, who also face rampant discrimination in our society and underrepresentation in our literature and libraries.

Since writing my 2014 book, I have learned a lot through the Targeting Autism forums, my own understanding of EDI, and my own reading and increased social and political awareness. I came to realize that there were things I would do differently now and that a major deficiency of the book was its lack of representation, since I had parents and professionals speak to the experience of autism rather than autistic people, for whom this was their lived experience.

Since I wrote the book, the autism world has also evolved. Previously accepted but problematic terminology has been largely abandoned, and the neurodiversity movement has grown along with the adoption of the social model of disability, which addresses the need to reduce barriers for autistic people so they can participate freely in society. It became clear to me, given the changes in the country, in libraries, and in myself, that a new edition of the book was needed.

However, even as more library programs and services became available for autistic young people, I became deeply concerned about what happens to them and to those with other disabilities as they age out of the educational system. I now wanted to spend my time shining a light on the needs of these adults and showing librarians what they could do to help fill the gap in services and programming for them. My mentor, collaborator, and friend Carrie Banks and I decided to write a book similar to my book about programming for autistic youth, but this one would be about adults, and so we pitched it to ALA Editions. The problem was that I couldn't both update the youth programming book and write the adult programming book, nor did I want to, much as I desired to see both happen.

Then I thought of Dr. Amelia Anderson, a knowledgeable and accomplished academic whose work focuses on the intersection of autism and libraries. I had met Dr. Anderson at the Targeting Autism forums, and I knew she would be the perfect person to research and write a new, updated edition of my 2014 book. And I was so right. I'm extremely grateful that when I approached Dr. Anderson to ask her if she would consider the project, she enthusiastically agreed on the spot. What you hold in your hands is the result, and Dr. Anderson has done me proud, updating the book in many ways and centering the voices of autism self-advocates in the conversation, where they are meant to be.

I hope that those of you who found my 2014 book useful are as pleased with this new edition as I am. And because I could trust Dr. Anderson with it, Carrie Banks and I had the opportunity to write our companion book, *Programming for Adults with Developmental Disabilities*. I hope your library will get and use that volume as well.

Acknowledgments

I AM ETERNALLY GRATEFUL TO THE COMMUNITY OF LIBRARIANS WHO shared program examples and best practices with me as I researched this book. In particular, the following librarians offered incredible insight.

Thanks to Heather Baucum, an incredibly dynamic school librarian in Virginia, for sharing about the incredible systems she has in place to support autistic students. Renee Grassi is a leader in inclusive library services, and the innovative work she has done contributed to this book significantly. Jen Taggart provided invaluable information about best practices for storytimes, as well as information about providing those services virtually. Erin Lovelace and Julia Frederick generously shared storytime examples, and Marie Plug shared examples from her library's blog. Thank you to Shelley Harris and Carrie Banks for sharing information about inclusive gardening and more. School librarians Katie Kier and Rachel LeClair generously shared examples of how they conduct successful programs. Along with a great team, Dianne Aimone conducted a series of successful programs with an "Autism Welcome Here" grant, and shared the results and program plans for inclusion in this book. I appreciate the time Ryan Moniz spent sharing with me about the teen and young adult programs he put into place. Anne Leon began some of the earliest sensory storytimes, and was happy to share her time with me to give updates on inclusive library programming. Holly Jin shared programming ideas and tips, and her successes at shifting programs online. Becky Fesler is doing incredible inclusive advocacy work at her library, and shared example program plans for families.

Of course, this book wouldn't have been possible without contributions from members and supporters of the autism community, in particular its contributors: Steph Diorio, Tina Dolcetti, Karen Stoll Farrell, Charlie Remy, "Justin Spectrum," Kate Thompson, Adriana White, Paul Wyss, and Heidi Zuniga. I'm grateful to be accepted as an ally, and hope that this edition is a step in the right direction toward acceptance and inclusion. Individual biographies of these contributors are provided at the end of the book.

Thank you also to my incredible students at Old Dominion University, who submitted case studies and ideas for best practices in libraries. You will find contributions from Sarah Brandow, Janet Coulson, Hope Hill Clark, Shannon Hoggatt, Karen Kinsey, Jessica Kompelien, Amber Langston, Jessica Lyszyk, and Reina Malakoff throughout the text.

I'm grateful to have had Jamie Santoro as an editor. She was always available to discuss progress and setbacks, and I was especially grateful for her guidance as I wrestled with my feelings of privilege and ally-ship. Jamie characterized my role in updating this book as being like the conductor of an autistic and allied orchestra—and I hope through this book that I've let all of these voices sing.

I can never thank Barbara Klipper enough for trusting me with making updates to her original work. I feel lucky to have been given such an excellent first edition to start from, and hope that my work on this second edition has made her proud.

Finally, I am so appreciative of my husband, Josh, who was incredibly encouraging as this book came together. I couldn't have done it without his support.

—*Amelia Anderson*

Introduction

I MET BARBARA KLIPPER FOR THE FIRST TIME AT THE "TARGETING AUTISM in Libraries" conference in 2018. As always, the event was inspiring and left me motivated to continue my work at the intersection of autism and libraries, bolstered by the self-advocates and allies I had met and learned from. On the final day of the conference, I noticed the name tag of the person behind me on the hotel shuttle—Barbara Klipper! This was a celebrity sighting for me, as I use and reference the first edition of her book often.

A few short months later, Barbara and I met again at the American Library Association (ALA) Annual Conference. She invited me to meet for coffee and a chat; little did I know that she had a bigger plan. After attending the "Targeting Autism in Libraries" conference and hearing from self-advocates, Barbara knew that her 2014 book needed a refresh. While the first edition accurately reflected the time in which it was published, there were new understandings and ideas that needed to be incorporated now. The book's language, terminology, and approaches needed to be updated to reflect the understanding of autism self-advocates, and to help librarians become true allies of the autistic youth in their communities. The book needed to include autistic voices themselves, and it needed to reflect the new knowledge that has been learned about autism, as well as new initiatives that libraries have introduced since the original publication. To my great honor, Barbara asked if I would take the lead on this update.

When we know better, we do better, and such is the case with this book. In this edition, I use the word "autistic" very purposefully, instead of referring to a child or teen as someone "with autism." This reflects the preferences of autistic self-advocates, who prefer identity-first, not person-first, language. This is an ongoing discussion, and I hope that no matter what your language preferences are, you will learn from the approaches provided in this book. A more nuanced discussion of language is provided in chapters 1 and 2.

When faced with updating this text, it was clear that the framing needed a major update. The program ideas provided in this book are incredibly rich and easy to replicate. My fear was that librarians would not read past the introductory chapters to access the program ideas, or else they would jump right to the program ideas and miss the reasons for the approaches suggested and the best practices to follow, which were covered in the first chapters of the first edition and are repeated here with some modification.

In this edition, there are now new, replicable programs and updates provided for the examples of successful library programming in the previous edition. But the work of programming must be grounded in general knowledge and an introduction to autism, and that information needs to be current and correct. This has all been updated with what we know today.

Additionally, we all experienced a monumental shift in 2020 with the COVID-19 pandemic. Library services shifted online, and many programs still operate this way. To account for these changes, I have included virtual options throughout the book. Look for the "Make It Virtual" tag within the chapters for ideas about programs that could easily be done in a virtual environment.

This edition will present the currently accepted facts about autism, and what are seen as best practices, but as you read you should keep a few things in mind:

1. Ideally, libraries should offer multiple, primarily inclusive programs, train staff repeatedly and in different ways, and apply all of the suggested best practices. However, we all live with budget and time constraints, and we must work within the mandates of our library administrations. As you read and apply the ideas presented in this book, feel free to modify them, both to match the autistic children and teens you serve and to fit your library's community and culture. Hopefully, if you have small successes, you will be able to build on them over time.

2. Our understanding of autism is constantly evolving, so what we know in 2021 may be seen as misguided in 2023. This continuous evolution is one reason for this second edition.

3. How autism is talked about may depend to some extent on who is doing the talking. Doctors and therapists, researchers, and parents may share common views about autism, or they may not. "Self-advocates," the term often used for autistic people who speak on their own behalf, may have a totally different concept of what autism is. This book will try to give you both the professional and the self-advocate view.

4. I have been careful to operate from the assumption that there is nothing about autism that needs to be "fixed" or feared, which is primarily the view of self-advocates and their allies. But there are educational needs to be addressed and barriers removed if we wish to improve services for the autistic members of the community.

This edition presents the facts as objectively as possible, while acknowledging that some of these facts are fluid and somewhat subjective. The aim is always to provide information and approaches that can improve library visits and programs for the autistic youth and teens you serve. This edition amplifies the voices of autistic self-advocates, all of whom are librarians themselves. Their voices were not included in the first edition, and that was a shortcoming of that book. It should be noted that these contributions were edited for length to be included in the printed text. These edits were made in careful collaboration with the authors, and no additional edits were made to change content, grammar, or otherwise alter the meaning of the original work.

I acknowledge my privilege as a non-autistic researcher, but I know that this privilege also allows me to provide a platform for those whose voices might otherwise not be heard. This edition amplifies the voices of autistic self-advocates, many of them librarians themselves. I am not autistic; I am a researcher, educator, and former public librarian. And as I hope I have demonstrated in this updated edition, I am also an ally.

There is still work to be done, but I hope that you find the second edition of this text even more approachable and valuable than the first. In the spirit of continual growth, I hope that you will reach out should you have questions or concerns about the approaches used in this text. Let's work together to move this conversation forward as we continually improve library services for the communities we serve.

—Amelia Anderson

How to Use This Book

AS BARBARA KLIPPER DESCRIBED IN THE FIRST EDITION, GIVEN THE prevalence of autism, there is a high price to pay when we avoid serving these community members and, by extension, their families. Every time an autistic child is not comfortable with or is unable to successfully use the library, that child's parents and siblings are not fully able to use this community resource either. These families are already isolated in many ways. We should not add to that isolation by effectively denying them access to one of our most important community institutions.

Our sincere hope is that this book will continue to provide librarians with a general comfort level, understanding of need, and easy-to-replicate ideas for successfully serving autistic children and teens in their communities.

Read the whole book, even if you think only one or two of the chapters apply to you. The material is arranged in a way that should be the most useful, but there is a lot of overlap. Many of the program ideas found in the chapter about schools, for example, can also work in a public library, and the introductory material in each chapter can also have broader applications.

The purpose of this book is to provide librarians who work with children and teens with enough information that they will no longer feel unprepared and fearful of working with autistic children and their families. Adults who work with young people in schools, community centers, and camps can also use the information and implement the programs found in this book

You'll learn a little about autism, including how it manifests in behaviors, as well as some general guidelines for interacting with autistic people in a library setting. We'll introduce the things you need to consider as you design programming for this population, we will describe best practices, and we'll tell you how to select books and music to use in your programs. We'll also supply programming ideas for different age groups, along with general information that can guide you as you apply or adapt those program ideas to your own library. Throughout the book and in the appendixes you'll encounter many useful resources: books, articles, websites, organizations, vendors, and possible funding sources that can assist you.

Does this sound like a lot for you to learn? Don't worry—it's not. The things that you need for success in programming for autistic young people and their families are a basic understanding of the issues; a knowledge of where to find resources, information, and support; and a big heart. If you are reading this, the odds are that you already have a big heart. You will have this book to refer to for the rest. The hope is that this book will help you feel confident enough to offer programs that serve these children and teens in your community.

What Is Autism?

Autism is considered a spectrum disorder because of the wide-ranging types and severity of characteristics that people with the disorder display. A quote commonly attributed to Dr. Stephen Shore, a professor and autistic self-advocate, is: "If you've met one person with autism, you've met one person with autism." The characteristics of autism manifest differently in every person with the disorder, and that is partly why the question, "What is autism?" is so hard to answer.

We can tell you what it is not. Autism is not a health crisis or a growing epidemic. It is something that is present in many of our children, family members, and peers—whether we realize it or not. Though often associated with children, autism is a lifelong disorder and can be diagnosed at any age. Some adults are diagnosed only when their children are evaluated for autism, and some adults we see as quirky or eccentric may actually be autistic and not realize it. However, even though diagnosis may not take place until later in life, autism falls under the umbrella of "developmental disorders" because it typically appears in childhood, and one does not suddenly become autistic later in life.

We won't provide the full picture here, but we will give you enough information about autism to help you design or adapt appropriate programs for members of the autism community. Read on.

What Does Autism Look Like in Children and Teens?

In general, autistic children look like . . . children. Autistic children do not have distinguishing facial characteristics. They are not necessarily bigger or smaller than other children. They do not use a wheelchair, braces, or other mobility aids because of their autism. Sometimes autistic children do call attention to themselves, but usually this is by their behavior, not their physical characteristics.

At some point you may have seen a child displaying what might seem like inappropriate behavior in your library or another public place: crying or screaming for no apparent reason, talking to themselves, spinning in circles, walking on their toes, or flapping their arms. The child may have stood too close to other people, not answered questions, refused to make eye contact, or walked away when someone addressed them. Their clothes may have been stained, chewed on, or torn, or their hair disheveled. And often their parent's repeated attempts to control them may have had no effect whatsoever. It's easy to assume that what you observed was an example of ineffective parenting, and while that may be true, it is equally possible, and perhaps more likely, that what you saw was an example of an autistic child who was not feeling comfortable. Many of those observable behaviors are actually the child's attempts to self-regulate. *Self-regulation* is the term for a person's ability to moderate their feelings when they are in situations that can provoke stress, anxiety, annoyance, or frustration.

You may see stimming behavior from children of any gender, not just boys. Statistics from the Centers for Disease Control (CDC) indicate that more boys than girls are diagnosed with autism spectrum disorder (ASD), but the truth is probably more complicated.[1] We can't be sure of the exact male-to-female ratio, and multiple theories exist as to why more males than females are diagnosed with ASD. While it is possible that males simply have a higher prevalence of autism, it might also be true that autism traits in females are underreported, that females are better at "masking" their differences, or that females have characteristics that don't fit within the traditional diagnostic criteria for autism. Some awareness of autism beyond the traditional male portrayal came in 2015, when *Sesame Street* introduced a female autistic puppet, Julia, on the popular program. (Note: While *Sesame Street* is still recommended as an excellent resource for autism education and materials, the Autistic Self Advocacy Network [ASAN] ended their partnership with *Sesame Street* in 2019 due to disagreements about their work with Autism Speaks.)[2]

Additionally, recent studies have revealed associations between autistic traits and gender variance, and a higher-than-average incidence of autistic people who also identify as GLBTQ.[3] For all of these reasons, the singular pronouns "they/them/theirs" are used throughout this text.

> ### What Is "Stimming"?
>
> You might see a child or teen "stimming" in your library, and wonder what is going on. *Stimming* refers to self-stimulatory behavior that results in the repetition of movements or sounds. It may manifest as hand-flapping, rocking, pacing, or using a fidget object. Stimming can help a person self-regulate, and if it is not causing harm to themselves or others, it can be an important tool for autistics.

AUTISM IN GIRLS
Karen Stoll Farrell

I can see a meltdown building in my nine-year-old daughter's eyes. We are at a new restaurant, and the menu choices are different than they were on the website that we reviewed before coming. Now she is full of fear and rage, her normally rational brain short-circuited. When she was five, my husband took her in for a diagnosis right after her older brother received his ASD diagnosis. We knew the bias against diagnosing girls with autism, but hoped that we had an edge as Autistic parents in explaining how her symptoms fit the spectrum. As it turned out, we were wrong.

The diagnostic criteria for autism, like many other medical diagnoses, were created over many years of working almost exclusively with boys. The current criteria are based very heavily on social skills and communication—which are, in turn, very heavily subjective and culturally created. As a society, we have recognized for decades now that we bring up girls and boys differently, especially in regard to how they communicate and socialize. The diagnostic criteria for autism do not recognize this difference.

Our now nine-year-old received a diagnosis of generalized anxiety. Upon receiving the explanation from the doctor's office, we discovered that she did meet the criteria for ASD, but that, in the doctor's "professional opinion", it was not the correct diagnosis. As it turns out, even when girls do meet the criteria, a doctor's bias can easily sweep all of that away.

We continue to feel the impact of this – it limits what insurance will cover, and it limits some social skills groups and camps that are specific about the need for an ASD diagnosis. However, these limitations are not the most difficult ones. The hardest ones stem from the ways in which our daughter presents differently from boys. She has always had difficult meltdowns, but almost exclusively at home, not out in public, and never at school; her inability to speak to strangers and her reticence in new environments are regularly written off as feminine "shyness"; her unwillingness to share toys, share in the creation of a game, and inability to understand social dynamics generally result in her quietly leaving a group of other children, rather than the outbursts of violence often seen in Autistic boys.

What all of this means is that she and we, as her parents, always have the burden of proof placed on us. From family members to teachers to strangers in restaurants and libraries, others look at our daughter and don't see that she is Autistic, opening the door for their judgment, and impacting further what assistance they are willing to offer our daughter.

Autism is lifelong. While we refer to autistic children and teens within this book, it is important to remember that those children and teens grow up— and are still autistic. Autism is not something that can be cured. While some autistic people develop strategies and approaches that help them better manage what might be uncomfortable manifestations of the disorder, autism does not go away. Though this book focuses on programming for children and teens, it will be helpful for you to remember that you are helping to provide supportive experiences for individuals who will grow up to be autistic adults. And just as with any other young library patrons, you are instilling a love of libraries at a young age, and building foundations for library use and patronage across the life span.

What Is Autism?

The Centers for Disease Control and Prevention (CDC) describes autism spectrum disorder (ASD) as "a developmental disability that can cause significant social, communication and behavioral challenges."[4]

In contrast, the Autistic Self Advocacy Network (ASAN) calls autism "a developmental disability that affects how we experience the world around us. Autistic people are an important part of the world. Autism is a normal part of life, and makes us who we are."[5] It is important to acknowledge both of these understandings of what autism "is."

The most comprehensive definition of autism can be found in the fifth edition of the *Diagnostic and Statistical Manual of Mental Disorders,* or *DSM-5,* a collection of criteria that mental health and insurance professionals rely on to diagnose various disorders. The *DSM-5* is published by the American Psychiatric Association and is revised periodically.

According to the *DSM-5,* the diagnostic criteria for autism spectrum disorder include:

1. Persistent deficits in social communication and social interaction across multiple contexts
2. Restricted, repetitive patterns of behavior, interests, or activities[6]

These are the shortened criteria, but they should give you enough information to provide a solid baseline of understanding. If you want more detail, you may be interested in viewing the full diagnostic criteria.

In *DSM-5,* several conditions that once were diagnosed individually became subsumed under the broader diagnosis of ASD. Three of these are the ones we most commonly encounter: autistic disorder, Asperger syndrome, and pervasive developmental disorder–not otherwise specified, or PDD-NOS (which is pretty much what the name sounds like). You might think of ASD now as the umbrella term for what were formerly separate diagnoses.

In recent years, it was common to refer to someone who had autism as a "person with autism." This is known as person-first language, and was used to reinforce the idea that the person is first and foremost a human being, and only in a secondary sense someone with a particular condition. By contrast, others use the terms "autistic person," "autistic individual," or (in the plural) "autistics" when referring to someone with the condition. This is known as identity-first language. While person-first language is still preferred by many other disability groups, autistic self-advocates and advocacy groups such as the Autistic Self Advocacy Network (ASAN) state their preference for identity-first language.

A Little History

Leo Kanner, a pediatric psychiatrist at the Johns Hopkins Hospital in Baltimore, was the first psychiatrist to clearly define autism. In "Autistic Disturbances of Affective Contact," a landmark paper published in 1943, Kanner described eleven boys he had seen in his practice, and observed that they demonstrated "an extreme autistic aloneness that whenever possible, disregards, ignores, shuts out anything that comes to the child from the outside."[7] Kanner noted that in addition to this extreme social isolation, the boys had a stronger attachment to objects than to people, displayed language and communication impairments, and had a strong aversion to change, obsessively needing everything in their world to remain constant. Kanner named this condition "early infantile autism," which later became known as "autism."

Autism was originally, and erroneously, thought to be a psychiatric condition related to schizophrenia. Kanner himself was an early proponent of this theory. He attributed his patients' characteristics to bad parenting, which he principally defined by the presence of "refrigerator mothers" who were so cold, distant, and unloving that their children had no choice but to retreat from the world. This incorrect theory dominated the field for decades and was spread widely by Bruno Bettelheim in *The Empty Fortress: Infantile Autism and the Birth of the Self* (1967).

At about the same time that Kanner was publishing his work, Hans Asperger, a psychiatrist in Vienna, Austria, was observing boys who had an inability to empathize with others, difficulty in forming friendships, clumsy movements, and an extreme obsession with a special interest. While similar in some ways to the children described by Kanner, the boys that Asperger studied tended to have higher levels of cognitive, social-emotional, and linguistic functioning. In 1981, the British psychiatrist Lorna Wing identified children displaying this group of characteristics as having Asperger's syndrome, a term that continued to be used until the publication of *DSM-5* in 2013.

One hero in the story of autism is Bernard Rimland, a psychologist with an autistic son. Rimland took exception to the bad-parenting theories and set out to debunk them. While Rimland is not widely known outside of the autism community, his contributions to the field were numerous and important. In *Infantile Autism: The Syndrome and Its Implications for a Neural Theory of Behavior* (1964) he promoted an alternative, biological explanation for autism. In addition to writing this classic, Rimland founded both the Autism Society of America (ASA) and the Autism Research Institute (ARI), and he supported many experimental treatments that eventually became accepted as the standard of care for autistic people.

Today professionals accept that autism is a neurobiological condition with a genetic component, and researchers are working to identify the biological, genetic, and environmental influences that cause the condition. Although we have seen much progress in this regard, there is much that is still not known.

Because there is no accurate test for autism and our knowledge of the condition's etiology is sketchy, neither professionals nor families always agree on all aspects of how to help autistic children. The only thing we can say for sure is that nobody yet knows the whole story, and that incorrect, destructive theories (like that of the "refrigerator mother") have demonstrated remarkable staying power. A more recent example of a long-lived and very harmful theory is the highly publicized idea that an additive in childhood vaccines causes autism. Although this conclusion was discredited with the admission that the original study was based on fraudulent data, it has refused to disappear from public view. The result is that some parents still believe it, refusing to vaccinate their children and creating significant public health consequences, such as the widespread measles outbreak in the United States in 2019.

What about Asperger Syndrome?

Arguably, an important transition from the *DSM-IV* (1994) to the *DSM-5* was the removal of Asperger syndrome as a stand-alone diagnosis.[8] This transition has led to some clunky decisions, and many are still wrestling with the aftermath. To differentiate those who were formerly given an Asperger's diagnosis from those who were autistic, "functioning" labels were briefly adopted by some. Thankfully, the terms "high-functioning" and "low-functioning" did not stick around for long, as they carry with them extremely negative connotations.

People who formerly identified as having an Asperger syndrome diagnosis must now make a conceptual shift to the broader diagnosis of autism spectrum disorder. While straightforward for some, others have had a hard time mapping their identities to a new diagnosis. You may hear some older teen or young adult patrons describe themselves as having Asperger syndrome. In all cases, we should let people identify how they choose. While it would be inaccurate now to design programming for individuals with Asperger syndrome, if a teen identifies as such, try to mirror their language.

What is generally accepted now is that ASD, or simply "autism," is the general term for anyone with an autism diagnosis, even those formerly diagnosed with Asperger syndrome. Assuming no major changes to future editions of the *DSM*, it is only a matter of time before the Asperger label disappears from the common vernacular.

WHO IS AN AUTISTIC PERSON?   *"Justin Spectrum"*

Who is an Autistic person? That person may have a formal diagnosis of autism spectrum disorder that is recognized by the *DSM-5*. However, autism is also an identity, which is why the term "Autistic" is being capitalized here. The formal diagnosis is so often necessary for educational or workplace accommodations, but can be quite expensive.

I was diagnosed as a 34-year-old adult, and the bill for my psychological testing and related report was over $3,000. I was fortunate enough to have premium health insurance, which reimbursed me for about two-thirds of this price tag under my out-of-network mental health coverage. Many therapists who diagnose and treat Autistics do not take insurance, and not everyone has out-of-network medical coverage or the resources to pay out of pocket and hope for a partial reimbursement. Due to these diagnosis and treatment barriers, many self-advocates argue that self-diagnosis or self-identification as Autistic should be considered valid.

While autism has historically been under-diagnosed, it has been well-documented that women and people of color are less likely to receive that diagnosis. Autism was initially identified in white men, and practitioners may be less likely to consider an autism diagnosis in a woman. The experience of Autistics of color has been narrated in an anthology called *All the Weight of Our Dreams: On Living Racialized Autism*. Lydia X. Z. Brown, in the introduction to this anthology, writes that "mainline autism and autistic organizations exist largely without us or with few autistics of color."[9] Brown also notes that nearly all major works on neurodiversity and Autistic politics have been produced by whites, with few contributions from Autistics of color.

Sensory Processing Disorders and Autism

The term *sensory processing* refers to the way our brains integrate the information we receive from our senses so that we can respond to it in physically or behaviorally appropriate ways. Most of this information comes to us through the familiar five senses (sight, hearing, touch, smell, and taste). We also get information from three additional senses: the proprioceptive (which allow us to know where we are in space and to have an idea of where our bodies begin and end), the vestibular (which tells us about our movement and balance), and the interoceptive (which provides information about what is going on internally in our bodies).

Sensory processing disorders (SPDs) are neurological conditions in which the body receives sensory information, but a neurological impairment prevents that information from being organized and interpreted by the brain in a way that results in inappropriate responses.

SPDs are extremely common; one recent study indicates that as many as one in twenty children may have some form of sensory processing disorder, while another study estimates that one in six children is affected.[10] And while there are children with SPD who are not also autistic, almost every autistic child has some degree of sensory processing disorder. In fact, in *DSM-5*, sensory processing issues are listed as one of the possible criteria for the diagnosis of ASD.

There are many ways that sensory processing disorders can affect the children and teens you see in your library:

- Sensitivity to tactile stimuli, indicated by resistance to certain textures, or discomfort with things like tags and seams in clothing. They may hate getting wet, touching clay or finger paint, or having dirty hands.
- Overreactions or underreactions to pain or noise.
- Sensory seeking, indicated by the child's need to touch everything, put things in their mouth, spin, or engage in other activities that give them lots of sensory input.
- Sensory avoidance, which is the opposite of sensory seeking. A child who feels bombarded by sensory input may seek out calm surroundings and become extremely distressed by crowds, noise, spicy foods, loud music, bright lights, or the touch of another person.
- Clumsiness, often manifested as stepping on toes or bumping into people or things. A child who has sensory discrimination problems may tear the paper when they write because they use too much force with their pen, pencil, or crayon.
- Poor motor planning, resulting from the inability to imagine a task, picture the steps needed, and then implement those steps in the correct sequence.
- Inability to follow directions, especially when the directions include more than a single step or action, or when they involve moving one's limbs across the midline of the body.
- Pain and frustration when the child cannot identify their physical feelings. For example, the child may know that their stomach hurts but can't determine whether they are hungry, have to go to the bathroom, or have another, more serious issue.

Because people with SPD can be either sensory avoiders or sensory seekers, you should be sure to offer sensory tools or activities that work for both groups. Calming activities and soft music will help sensory avoiders, but they will do nothing for those in need of sensory stimulation.

Autism Is a Disability

In this book, we mostly talk about autism in isolation, but it is important to remember that autism is a recognized disability, and autistic people are therefore included in more general disability-related laws and policies.

WHO IS A DISABLED PERSON UNDER U.S. LAW?

"Justin Spectrum"

Autism is a disability. It is defined as such under precedents in U.S. civil rights and education law going back to the 1970s, when laws were passed that were the predecessors of the Americans with Disabilities Act (ADA) and the Individuals with Disabilities in Education Act (IDEA) of 1990. An American is considered to be disabled under a "three-pronged" definition: if they have a physical or mental impairment that substantially limits one or more major life activities, have a record (i.e., medical documentation) of such an impairment, or are regarded as having such an impairment.[11] The ADAAA (ADA Amendments Act) of 2008 expanded the list of "major life activities" whose impairment constitutes disability, and added "major bodily functions" to this umbrella.[12]

IDEA and a series of court rulings over the past forty-five years have defined the concepts of a "free appropriate public education" (FAPE) and the "least restrictive environment" (LRE), and required disabled students to have an "individualized education plan" (IEP).[13] Youth services library workers should familiarize themselves with these concepts and may find them applicable when planning programs to best include Autistic children and teens.

I was diagnosed with autism spectrum disorder, severity level 1 (what would have once been termed "Asperger's syndrome") as an adult. I have received no accommodations at any level of education, or in any workplace. Yet, under the three-pronged definition (discussed above), I am disabled. I have been diagnosed with a condition that impairs major life activities and bodily functions, and I have a record of this impairment: the report from my psychological testing.

The aforementioned ADAAA of 2008's expanded list of "major life activities" includes communicating, speaking, and concentrating, all of which are impaired in some way by my autism. (Even though I am a speaking Autistic who deals with the public, I still have challenges with communication.) Furthermore, neurological and brain functions are considered major bodily functions. I am disabled under U.S. law as at least two of the prongs in the well-established definition apply to me, and autism has consistently been considered to be a disability under EEOC (Equal Employment Opportunity Commission) guidelines.

Along with these legal boundaries, one should consider the viewpoint of Autistic self-advocates. Amythest Schaber, in their *Ask an Autistic* series on their YouTube channel, explains why autism is a disability in episode 16. Some may not want to consider Autistics to be disabled because there may be a stigma attached to the term *disability*. However, autism is a disability from a medical and legal viewpoint and by the consensus of self-advocates. While one can easily find T-shirts online declaring that autism is not a disability but a "difference" or a "superpower," a deeper understanding of disability itself will encourage autism acceptance and even pride.

Neurodiversity

The neurodiversity movement is a phenomenon you should be aware of because it pertains to autism. In the 1990s Judy Singer, a sociologist and autistic self-advocate, coined the term *neurodiversity* to represent variations in the human brain. As this term continues to gain popularity, you might hear it used interchangeably with *autism*, which is not entirely correct. While autism is one form of neurodiversity, other neurological conditions or disorders such as attention deficit hyperactivity disorder (ADHD), dyslexia, and Tourette's syndrome also fall under the neurodiversity umbrella. The neurodiversity movement operates under the assumption that neurological variations are not flaws, but instead should be seen as diversity. The movement also draws from elements of the social model of disability, which essentially claims that a person is disabled when society presents barriers to make it so. This is a complex set of theories and thoughts, and we don't want to overwhelm you with too much detail here. If you want to further your knowledge, there are many resources you can easily find that can provide more information about both neurodiversity and the social model of disability.

LIBRARY SERVICES THROUGH A DISABILITY STUDIES LENS   *"Justin Spectrum"*

The field of disability studies positions disability as being first and foremost socially constructed. Impairment (e.g., a wheelchair user's mobility impairment) is real; disability is the result of a world that is not designed for people with those impairments. To look at autism and Autistic people through a "disability studies lens" offers a clear path to acceptance. Why can't Autistic people fully participate in your library? Should the structure of the library itself, the facilities and policies, be examined more for their role in constructing barriers?

Surely, you are "aware" of autism. That awareness may lead you to recommend a book like *Rules* (2006) by Cynthia Lord, which was positively reviewed at the time and earned a Newbery Honor. Riki Entz, writing for the *Disability in Kidlit* blog in 2015, offered a different perspective. *Rules* is the story of Catherine, the non-Autistic sibling; David, her Autistic brother, is mostly a plot device. David's parents don't respond to him when he communicates through echolalia (repetitive speech), and scold Catherine for doing so. David's way of communicating is not treated as valid, and indeed there are few attempts in the book to humanize him. The title of the book is a reference to Catherine making "rules" for David to discourage behaviors that she finds embarrassing. A main theme of the book is Catherine's wish that she had a "normal" brother, and her desire to change him.[14]

Steve Silberman's *NeuroTribes: The Legacy of Autism and the Future of Neurodiversity* (2015) pushed the idea of autism as a civil rights issue into the popular consciousness. Silberman wrote "the idea of neurodiversity has inspired the creation of a rapidly growing civil rights movement based on the simple idea that the most astute observers of autistic behavior are autistic people themselves rather than their parents or doctors."[15]

The autism self-advocacy movement has positioned itself in the disability rights tradition; the term itself is borrowed from the disability rights movement.[16] The self-advocacy movement positions many of the barriers experienced by Autistic people as socially constructed, and neurodiversity is a cousin of autism self-advocacy. The use of identity-first language, e.g., Autistic person instead of person with autism, is borrowed from Deaf activists.[17]

The Evolution of Symbols

You might be familiar with the puzzle piece as a commonly used symbol to represent autism. This imagery developed from Britain's National Autistic Society in 1963, and grew to represent autism as it was adopted by organizations, publishers, and more. As recognizable as this symbol is, it is no longer thought of as positive imagery within the autistic community. Autistic people are not puzzling, nor are they incomplete and in need of being made whole, as the puzzle piece imagery suggests. Recently, there has been a shift by major autism research journals and self-advocates from the puzzle piece to the infinity symbol, which represents neurodiversity more broadly.

FIGURE 1.1
Neurodiversity symbol

About the Increase in Prevalence

You may be aware that the prevalence of autism has been steadily increasing in recent years. In 2000, the Centers for Disease Control reported a prevalence of

ASD of one in every 150 children in the United States. The analysis of data from a 2014 study showed a jump to the most recent rate of one in every fifty-four children meeting the diagnostic criteria for ASD.[18] Does this mean that autism is more prevalent than ever before in our country? Maybe, but probably not. What is more likely the cause for this apparent jump is that public awareness has increased, the diagnostic criteria have widened, and we are simply able to more accurately identify what has always been present. So autism is not an epidemic, but it is definitely being diagnosed more frequently. These statistics are just one part of the story, but they do mean that every librarian is likely to encounter autistic people in their library and community.

The Library's Role

By their very design, libraries are already great places for many autistic people to explore their interests, find community, and just hang out. However, there is always room for improvement. As librarian Kate Thompson says: "I was inspired to go to graduate school for my MLIS after watching my autistic son struggle to attend storytime at our local library. I wanted to study how programs could best be tailored for a variety of needs." With more knowledge about autism and inclusion, librarians can address barriers and provide even more supportive services and programming for autistic people.

THE LIBRARY AS A SANCTUARY
Heidi Zuniga

There are two important, intersecting arcs in my life: libraries and autism. Libraries figured into my life well before I knew anything about autism, or that libraries and autism intersect. Autism entered my life four years ago when one of my children was diagnosed, followed by another.

The connection between autistics and libraries is not mysterious. The library could be viewed through an autistic lens as a place where logically ordered information about any topic of interest is housed in a quiet, welcoming place—a place that requires very little "social performance" to access. Additionally, it has been suggested that autism may be highly represented among library staff—many of whom may not be aware of their status, but who have always found libraries to be a comfortable fit personally and professionally. Until very recently, those on the subtler end of the autism spectrum would likely have gone undiagnosed. Today, with our better understanding of autism, we know many autistics "pass" as neurotypical. They can nevertheless still face challenges such as sensory issues, social difficulties, and frequent anxiety.

I spent a lot of time in public libraries when I was growing up, mostly looking for books on horses and dogs, or just reading. I pursued a career in librarianship once I discovered librarians were my "tribe." Library work was not only interesting, but I was good at it. Predictably, I bring my children to the public library often, and it seems to be a place they enjoy as much as I do. For them, it isn't just the books about animals, the novels by J. R. R. Tolkien, or whatever their special interest is at that time—it is also the space itself. My children feel completely accepted and valued in the library. One of them particularly likes the behavioral rules and expectations posted on the wall for everyone to see. They love the shadowy nooks, sunny window coves, and fascinating pieces of furniture they can burrow into along with their books. It is also quiet in the library, and the light is neither too bright nor too dim. Whatever questions (or monologues) my children might pose to a librarian are never met with the strained, disapproving looks they sometimes get from other adults. Instead, they are received with kindness, and professionalism. For us, libraries are a sanctuary.

Libraries are a special place for many autistics, and likely always will be. I encourage library staff to become more informed about the ways in which autism and libraries can intersect. Keep autism in mind as you design your spaces, programs, and collections. But, also keep doing what you already do so well: supporting those earnest, idiosyncratic regulars who probably memorized the call numbers and shelf locations where their beloved books can be found.

Final Thoughts

Feeling overwhelmed? Relax. Remember: you don't have to be an expert to work with these children and teens, and each chapter will give you more information to guide you. The autistic children and teens you work with can give you clues to what they need if you learn how to communicate with them and listen to them. Their parents and professionals are also available to provide you with information and support. For example, many children who have been identified as autistic or who have sensory processing issues work with sensory integration occupational therapists in their schools or privately. These therapists can be a valuable resource for you if you want to know more about SPD or how to incorporate activities that promote sensory integration into your programs.

NOTES

1. Jon Baio et al., "Prevalence of Autism Spectrum Disorder among Children Aged 8 Years—Autism and Developmental Disabilities Monitoring Network, 11 Sites, United States, 2014," *MMWR Surveillance Summaries* 67, no. 6 (2018): 1.

2. "ASAN Has Ended Partnership With Sesame Street," Autistic Self Advocacy Network (ASAN), August 5, 2019, https://autisticadvocacy.org/2019/08/asan-has-ended-partnership-with-sesame-street/.

3. Naisha A. Nabbijohnet al., "Gender Variance and the Autism Spectrum: An Examination of Children Ages 6–12 Years," *Journal of Autism and Developmental Disorders* 49, no. 4 (2019): 1570–85.

4. Centers for Disease Control and Prevention (CDC), "Autism Spectrum Disorder (ASD)," www.cdc.gov/ncbddd/autism/facts.html.

5. Autistic Self Advocacy Network, "About Autism," https://autisticadvocacy.org/about-asan/about-autism/.

6. American Psychiatric Association, *Diagnostic and Statistical Manual of Mental Disorders (DSM-5)* (Arlington, VA: American Psychiatric Publications, 2013).

7. Leo Kanner, "Autistic Disturbances of Affective Contact," *Nervous Child* 2 (1943): 217–50.

8. American Psychiatric Association, DSM-5.

9. Lydia X. Z. Brown, "Introduction: Notes from the Field (Not the Ivory Tower)," in *All the Weight of Our Dreams: On Living Racialized Autism,* by Lydia X. Z. Brown, E. Ashkenazy, and Morenike Giwa Onaiwu (DragonBee, 2017), 5.

10. Roianne Ahn et al., "Prevalence of Parents' Perceptions of Sensory Processing Disorders among Kindergarten Children," *American Journal of Occupational Therapy* 58, no. 3 (2004): 287–93. See also A. Ben-Sasson, A. S. Carter, and M. J. Briggs-Gowen, "Sensory Over-Responsivity in Elementary School: Prevalence and Social-Emotional Correlates," *Journal of Abnormal Child Psychology* 37 (2009): 705–76. Both articles can be accessed at www.spdfoundation.net.

11. U.S. Equal Employment Opportunity Commission, "Questions and Answers."

12. U.S. Equal Employment Opportunity Commission, "ADA Amendments Act of 2008" (section 4, "Disability Defined and Rules of Construction"), September 25, 2008, www.eeoc.gov/statutes/ada-amendments-act-2008.

13. *Endrew F. v. Douglas County School District Re-1*, 137 S. Ct. 988 (2016).

14. Riki Entz, "Review of *Rules* by Cynthia Lord," *Disability in Kidlit*, April 12, 2015, http://disabilityinkidlit.com/2015/04/12/review-rules-by-cynthia-lord/.

15. Steve Silberman, *NeuroTribes: The Legacy of Autism and the Future of Neurodiversity* (New York: Avery, an Imprint of Penguin Random House, 2015) 22.

16. Silberman, *NeuroTribes*.

17. Silberman, *NeuroTribes*.

18. Matthew J. Maenner, "Prevalence of Autism Spectrum Disorder among Children Aged 8 Years – Autism and Developmental Disabilities Monitoring Network, 11 Sites, United States, 2016," *Surveillance Summaries* 69, no. 4 (March 2020):1–12, http://dx.doi.org/10.15585/mmwr.ss6904a1.

Decisions to Make

A LIBRARY PROGRAM CAN BE DESIGNED WITH ALL THE BEST INTEN-
tions, but unless your library embraces a culture of inclusion, autistic
children, teens, and their families will not feel welcome there. While
there are many considerations you will want to take into account well before
you begin planning the content of your programs, perhaps the two most important things you will want to think about are the following:

1. How will you create and support a culture of inclusion?
2. How will you train and educate staff to support this mission?

This chapter will address those concerns.

Creating a Culture of Inclusion

Families need to feel welcome in your programs, and that starts with creating
a culture of inclusion—both in your programs and in your library as an institution. If a child has a positive experience in a program but is misunderstood and
conflict arises while checking books out or using the library computers, that
child's family may not feel welcome at the library. It is critical that your library
support understanding and inclusion in all areas of the library and with all personnel. How can you begin to develop a culture of inclusion in your library so
that parents and caregivers feel more comfortable bringing their autistic children to general library programs and for library visits? So that autistic teens feel
welcome to join their neurotypical peers at the library?

You should think about creating a diversity and inclusion task force and pol-
icy to address these issues. Think about ways to celebrate and normalize autism
all year, not just in April, which is Autism Acceptance month. Think about ways
to adjust your programming environment to facilitate inclusion. Think about
providing sensory tools at public service desks, and quiet spaces in the library.
Think about ways you can provide space in your programs for children and

teens to "stim," or use self-stimulating behaviors, to manage their response to sensory overload. It is important to move beyond autism awareness to autism acceptance. As librarian Holly Jin says, "[their] participation might look different, but it doesn't mean [an autistic child] is enjoying your library program any less than their peers."

A WELL-ROUNDED APPROACH TO ACCEPTING AUTISTICS IN THE LIBRARY   *"Justin Spectrum"*

There is no simple answer as to how to make Autistic kids and teens feel welcome in a public library. Collections matter; you should have a healthy mix of #ownvoices books for kids and teens. You should offer parenting books that are geared toward acceptance, not "cures" and misinformation. Attitudes matter; libraries can be places with strict "behavioral expectations." An Autistic person who experiences echolalia, or struggles to modulate their voice, may not meet these behavioral expectations. Indeed, not every person's information-seeking behavior may fit your expectations.

That Autistic child who comes to your program may appear to be disruptive, but if you provide them with an accepting space, that program could be super-meaningful to them. As youth services librarians, it's easy to be self-critical and perfectionist in evaluating our own programs. Sometimes, providing that accepting space is the most valuable aspect of any program! If an Autistic child or teen sees your library as a safe, comfortable place, your program is a success!

Universal Design

One way to incorporate inclusive practices to support not just autistic patrons, but everyone you serve, is through the principles of universal design. You might have heard about this term, but perhaps you don't know what it means for you as a librarian. First, we will explore the concept itself, and then we'll unpack what this means for you as you develop and implement programs.

Universal design is a concept first developed in 1997 within the field of architecture and design. Since its conception, universal design has grown to have broad implications for nearly any product or environment. As established by its original authors, universal design is "the design of products and environments to be usable by all people, to the greatest extent possible, without the need for adaptation or specialized design."[1]

One example of universal design can be found in librarian Renee Grassi's update of the Youth Department at the Glen Ellyn (IL) Public Library. She selected a variety of seating options, including "active seating" that allows children and teens to wobble. For an autistic child who needs active physical

The Seven Principles of Universal Design

1. *Equitable use:* The design is useful and marketable to people with diverse abilities.
2. *Flexibility in use:* The design accommodates a wide range of individual preferences and abilities.
3. *Simple and intuitive use:* Use of the design is easy to understand, regardless of the user's experience, knowledge, language skills, or current concentration level.
4. *Perceptible information:* The design communicates necessary information effectively to the user, regardless of ambient conditions or the user's sensory abilities.
5. *Tolerance for error:* The design minimizes hazards and the adverse consequences of accidental or unintended actions.
6. *Low physical effort:* The design can be used efficiently and comfortably and with a minimum of fatigue.
7. *Size and space for approach and use:* Appropriate size and space are provided for approach, reach, manipulation, and use regardless of the user's body size, posture, or mobility.

engagement during a program, these chairs are a great option, and they are fun for other children as well.

Universal design goes hand-in-hand with the idea of inclusion because you are creating an environment that is more universally accessible to all library patrons. For us, this means a more naturally inclusive environment for autistic children and teens, obviating the need for segregation or unnecessary disclosure. Think about autistic children and teens who might not yet have a diagnosis, or those who might not be neurodivergent but would simply benefit from a more comfortable, efficient programming environment. Finally, think about older autistic youth or teens who simply want to enjoy a library program with their peers, and prefer not to "other" themselves by disclosing a diagnosis. They would still benefit greatly from an environment that better supports them. Designing inclusive, more universally accommodating programs will benefit a greater segment of the community you work with.

Throughout this book, we provide you with suggestions and tips for providing services specifically for autistic children and teens. However, we also strongly encourage you to think about making all library services more accessible to everyone, in accordance with the principles of universal design. Programming specifically for the autistic user group is important, but it is equally essential to make sure that people of all abilities feel welcome, accepted, and served well in all library offerings.

UNIVERSAL DESIGN FOR LIBRARIES   *Adriana White*

My time in libraries inspired me to become a librarian, and it was during my MLIS work that I received my autism diagnosis. In all the libraries I visited in my childhood, none of those librarians ever knew I was autistic. Nevertheless, they still provided sensory-friendly spaces where I could safely read and learn—just as librarians today do for autistic patrons all over the United States.

It is no surprise that libraries are a favorite place for many autistics. Libraries are a great place to research special interests. They have quiet study rooms, are orderly and organized, and have copious amounts of signage.

These factors are great examples of universal design.

Broadly put, universal design encourages the creation of environments that fulfill the needs of many diverse groups all at once, instead of creating separate and segregated spaces for different needs. When done well, universal design benefits all patrons, and minimizes the amount of direct effort required to meet unique user needs. For example, curb cuts on sidewalks are not only useful for wheelchairs users—they also benefit parents with strollers, skateboarders, and elderly walkers. In a similar fashion, the accommodations that libraries provide autistic patrons can benefit many patrons.

Some examples of accommodations that libraries can provide are:

Physical Accommodations

- Flexible seating and work options
- Distinct spaces of varying sound and light levels (quiet rooms and sensory rooms)
- Sensory kits (noise-canceling headphones, fidgets, etc.)
- Clear and specific signage

Technological Accommodations

- Computers with accessibility options (screen readers, predictive text, etc.)
- Materials in multiple formats (books, e-books, audiobooks)
- Posting information, such as schedules and policies, online
- Captioning videos on the library website
- Offering recordings and transcripts of important events
- Providing virtual tours on the library website

The simplest and most impactful accommodations that libraries can provide are distinct spaces, clear signage, and sensory kits.

The noise levels in a library can vary greatly, depending on its programming. Offering distinct spaces, such as quiet rooms and sensory rooms, can greatly benefit patrons. Autistics can have complicated auditory needs. Many will not want to hear a lot of noise, but will occasionally make noise themselves—especially when stimming. However, many autistics do not tolerate or enjoy absolute silence, either.

Clear and specific signage in libraries is one of my most frequently used accommodations. Social interactions can be overwhelming, so being able to use a map, a schedule, or a digital catalog can be a lifesaver. Libraries can present this information in several ways—on signs, in a slideshow on a monitor, or on their website. Pairing text with images will make signage easier to comprehend and more accessible to autistic patrons, while also benefiting patrons who struggle with reading, or whose primary language is not English. Using high-contrast, large text, and color-coding can also benefit patrons with visual impairments, while increasing comprehension for autistics. Additionally, I always appreciate libraries that post important information online. Viewing this information to plan my visit beforehand helps ease my anxiety about going someplace new.

Sensory kits are another simple yet effective accommodation. These kits include items such as noise-canceling headphones and fidgets. Patrons can pick up and return a kit without interacting with library staff, and the kits are available to any patron who wishes to use them.

Universal Design for Learning

You might have also heard about Universal Design for Learning (UDL), and be confused about the difference between UDL and UD. Universal Design for Learning is designed primarily for educators and learning materials, not for physical spaces and objects, as universal design is. But like UD, UDL can easily be applied to libraries in the informal learning situations that make up library programs.

UDL has three principles:

1. Provide multiple means of engagement.
2. Provide multiple means of representation.
3. Provide multiple means of action and expression.[2]

UDL principles can be incorporated in the materials you use in your programs, the outputs, and the way you give directions. For example, you can introduce stories in multiple ways, such as through the physical book and reading aloud. You can use multiple communication styles, such as visual, auditory, and ASL signing, to increase the likelihood that your message will be received and processed by all. When you give directions, say them, demonstrate them visually, and model them physically. This gives children multiple opportunities to understand what you want them to do. In arts or crafts programs, provide projects with different degrees of difficulty, or let the children create a variety of possible items from the available materials, giving them multiple means of expression. If you plan to implement programming that is directly instructional and are interested in learning more about how to apply UDL principles, we encourage you to explore these concepts further through the CAST website (www.cast.org).

EQUITABLE ACCESS   *Adriana White*

Beyond physical accommodations, libraries can also offer patrons intangible supports. Universal Design for Learning encourages multiple means of access, engagement, and expression. In libraries, equitable access includes materials in multiple formats, as previously noted. Libraries should also offer multiple methods of communicating with staff (in-person, chat, e-mail, social media, comment boxes, etc.). These accommodations will be consistently utilized by more than just autistic patrons.

Staff can also support patrons by being patient and flexible. Give patrons ample time to find the words they need to say, and give them plenty of processing time to respond to your questions. Be compassionate and kind when dealing with social issues. Be sure to support the special interests of your individual patrons whenever possible!

An inclusive library that welcomes and celebrates diverse patrons can inspire its community. Neurodivergent patrons, English language learners, and disabled patrons are a part of every community, and their needs can be met in our libraries without stigmatization or fear, while simultaneously improving the lives of all our patrons. After all, libraries are for everyone.

Staff Training

Having many librarians and staff members in your organization invested in an inclusive mission is critical for your programming success for multiple reasons. Children and families should have an enjoyable experience using all library spaces and resources, not just when in a program room. This means that all staff they encounter should be educated about providing appropriate services and support. As librarian Renee Grassi says: "Training is the first place to start. You can do all the programming you want, but if they head to the front desk and then they're not having inclusive experiences, everything you're doing in programming is for naught." Awareness about autism is a good first step, but it needs to go one step further to acceptance. Training should include a strong emphasis on letting children and teens be themselves, and library staff should understand and accept those behaviors as long as the patrons are not putting themselves or others at risk.

Additionally, offering training more than once and in more than one way is important for continuity when there are staff changes. Librarians often change roles, both within and outside of their organization. Families who are used to a welcoming environment should not have to disrupt their routines due to changing library staff. By having all library staff educated about autism, you can

Communication Strategies

An important topic to cover in staff training is basic communication strategies that make interactions easier for everyone. Think about the following:

- Autistic people are concrete, literal thinkers. Because of this, you should be prepared to hear the honest truth. Although this might initially lead to hurt feelings, once you understand that this is just a communication style, it becomes truly refreshing.
- Along those lines, try to avoid using slang, idioms, and other figurative language.
- Try using visual supports, which can be very helpful to support communication.
- When giving directions or instructions, present one step at a time.
- Provide very clear directions. Focus on the behavior you wish to see rather than what not to do. Remember, be straightforward and honest.

- Don't expect an autistic person to make eye contact or to show body language that indicates they are paying attention. These social cues are not innate for them, and the child gazing at their shoe might be paying just as much attention as the child nodding their head in agreement.
- Non-speaking children likely have a preferred method of "augmented and alternative communication" (AAC); one common example is the Picture Exchange Communication System (PECS). Ask the child's parent or caregiver for guidance, and use the child's preferred method to communicate.
- Don't forget that autistic people like to interact and engage just as much as anyone else; they just might have a different communication style. Provide options for communication so that they can participate in the way that best suits them.

ensure that this culture of inclusion will be consistent throughout the library or system, and will persist through personnel changes.

All library personnel will benefit from knowing how to communicate more effectively with autistic people. Interactions can be made easier if library personnel understand more about the general characteristics and manifestations of autism, and are willing to adapt or bend some rules and provide guidelines in order to facilitate library visits.

You should share the ideas and some of the characteristics of autism that we cover in this book with your library's staff. If you choose to offer more formal training or workshops on topics such as assistive technology (AT), look to your school district's special education department, a local university, or a local autism organization to find presenters or facilitators. Reach out to the local branch of ASAN or similar organizations to identify self-advocates who can speak to your staff and introduce autism from their unique perspective. Many excellent resources and training opportunities can be found online, and in "Appendix A: Training and Education" at the end of this book.

Remember that training should not be a one-time event, but instead an ongoing occurrence for library staff.

SERVING CHILDREN ON THE AUTISM SPECTRUM
Shannon Hoggatt

According to ALA's Code of Ethics, the first tenet is to provide equitable service policies, equitable access, and unbiased, courteous responses to all requests. ALA's Library Bill of Rights likewise states that "a person's right to use a library should not be abridged because of origin, age, background, or views."[3] Any reasonable accommodations that can be made for a patron with a disability must be made, not only according to ethics but according to the Americans with Disabilities Act.

There is no one perfect way to serve children on the autism spectrum because it presents so differently in everyone. It is therefore vital for a library to show flexibility and patience to these patrons. One concrete step that can be taken is to "provide very obvious signage alerting [patrons] to which sections are quiet and in which sections communication and socialization are allowed."[4]

Aside from this, it is vital that librarians increase their awareness of autism spectrum disorder by taking advantage of online training modules, as "awareness is the first step towards tailoring the environment" and "providing access to resources"[5] for all patrons. Our continuing mission as librarians is to educate ourselves alongside of our communities on all issues that affect them.

Pre-Programming Decisions

Once you have established how you will approach the concerns already discussed in this chapter, you can begin to think about your programs themselves. But before you can plan content, you will have to make some decisions. Many of these decisions, like deciding on your source of funding and what ages to include in your programs, are ones you probably make for every program you offer. But they may be more nuanced in developing programming for autistic children and teens. Some questions you will want to ask yourself include:

- What are your goals for the program?
- Will your program be inclusive or autism-specific?
- What age range are you targeting?
- How will you market the program?
- What kind of budget will the program require, and what funding is available?
- What frequency, time, and length of program do you envision?
- Will you collaborate with other organizations?
- How will you evaluate the program?

The subsections below provide some information that can help you answer these questions.

Program Goals

Library programs are often evaluated in terms of the number of participants they attract. This doesn't always work for programs that serve autistic people, which are often more successful with a smaller audience and the opportunity for more personal attention. If head count isn't the goal, think about what is. Realistic goals for your programs may include letting all families know they are welcome at the library, allowing children the opportunity to come as they are, helping children feel supported through inclusive structures at regular library programs, providing a safe space for children who need extra space to move during library events, offering social opportunities for children and teens to interact with their peers, and providing a place for families to meet and network.

You should survey your community to determine what they want from their library. Sometimes we have an idea of what we might like to do, but it doesn't align with our community's actual needs. Know the "why" of your programming goals, and plan with those goals in mind from the very beginning.

Inclusive or Autism-Specific Programming

The term *inclusion* refers to the practice of integrating children with disabilities into classrooms, programs, and events alongside their neurotypical peers. Many libraries offer inclusive programming, utilizing practices that support autistic children and teens in programs that are open to all. The inclusive approach to programming has many benefits—it encourages autistic children to socialize with others they will encounter in school, and it encourages other children to be more accepting of differences. Both groups will learn from each other. Additionally, inclusion allows you to serve a larger portion of the population with your programs.

On the other hand, even in an inclusive library environment, you might still want to plan some programs specifically for autistic children or teens. These are *autism-specific* programs. Maybe you have a class visiting your public library for a field trip, and you know all the attendees will be autistic. Maybe you want to provide a special storytime to help autistic kids gain familiarity with the library before they attend a larger, inclusive group there. Or maybe you have an autistic group that already meets regularly in your library, and you want to do more to offer support. Sometimes the parents of autistic children request autism-specific library programs because they feel more comfortable in a setting where they know that others will understand their child's behavior. Though we always recommend inclusive practices, there will be situations in which a program just for autistic kids or teens might be most appropriate. Remember, though, that children and teens attending these programs should feel just as welcome and comfortable outside of the program room as they do within it. If you do decide to offer autism-specific programming, this should not be in lieu of implementing inclusive strategies in your other services or promoting other library offerings to these users.

One option is to start younger children in autism-specific programs and move them into more inclusive programs as they become more comfortable with the library. Of course, the ideal is to offer both types of programming and then determine the value and effectiveness of each type.

Identifying Ages for Your Program

In general, it is better to keep the age range of the participants in a program fairly narrow, regardless of their ability level. Like most children, autistic children like to be with their peers, and they prefer materials designed for their own age group. An older child or teen who cannot read material at grade level may not respond well to picture books designed for young children. They may, however, be quite engaged if you use magazines, picture books aimed at older readers, graphic novels, or heavily illustrated coffee-table books.

Cognitive, social, and verbal abilities manifest differently in every autistic person, however. Limiting programs by age might limit some participants who fall just outside of that age range but would enjoy the program's content. This is an area in which we suggest you establish a general age range for your programs, but remain flexible based on the circumstances. For example, while it would be inappropriate to allow a group of teenagers to join your preschool sensory storytime, you might allow an older child to attend instead of turning them away. You should try to provide a positive experience for all potential participants, and be prepared to make these decisions on an individual basis.

Outreach and Marketing

Libraries typically promote programs through newsletters and websites, and through flyers and brochures available at the library. These methods, though, are geared toward current library users, and may not be sufficient to get the word out to many of the autistic people you are targeting. If they are not already library users, or if they have had a bad experience at a library where staff were not welcoming or knowledgeable about autism, they are probably not looking at the library's publicity materials. Librarian Renee Grassi, who has years of experience, describes how she gains the trust of autistic attendees: "It took us a long time to get a steady group of attendees. If they have had a bad experience, it takes a long time [for them] to be trusting again. People can think of the library as an institution, but not as a welcoming place. Everything I do [in marketing our programs] I want to know how we can do better. We may not have been welcoming in the past, but how can we do better? It takes starting from a real place, and knowing that we don't think we've always done it right."

Be creative in reaching out to other resources in your community. Grassi says: "We have to recognize that people don't always feel safe in our spaces. We have to figure out why and address it. This means going outside your library and meeting parents at their special education PTO meetings. Telling them what you're doing, but also listening."

Once you've established a relationship with them, the special education department in your school district, social service agencies, parent support groups, and speech and occupational therapists in private practice may be happy to distribute your flyers. You can use or create e-mail distribution lists to send out e-mail blasts announcing new programs or reminding frequent attendees of ongoing ones. Grassi says: "It's about visibility and goodwill. [Autistic] people have a right to be at the library too. Social services, public health, and special education teachers—they're the gateway to a lot of relationships with kids. They can promote directly to parents in an e-mail."

Local websites for the families of children with disabilities can promote your programs and can also provide valuable information about other resources, so it's worth investigating if there is such a group in your area. Meetup.com is a good place to look for local groups you can send library information to, and you might also find local communities through Facebook and Nextdoor. Think outside the box for promoting your programs, since many autism families may not yet realize that the library has programs specifically designed to include them.

For those families who are already library users, work on strengthening those connections as well. As Grassi says, "if you know someone with autism who goes to your library—their network is small but it's powerful. When people realize you're a welcoming place, word will get out."

Grassi says that marketing autism programs is all about building trust and relationships. It is a multipronged approach that does not happen quickly, or by doing just one thing. She describes it as a "slow burn" as people get to know what you're doing, and spread the word that librarians are providing programming "from an authentic place."

Outreach to Underrepresented Groups

Autism can affect anyone and does not discriminate on the basis of income, education, gender, sexual identity, race, religion, or country of origin. It is important to not only provide programs that serve all groups, but also to ensure that traditionally marginalized communities are aware of your offerings—these are often the children who will benefit the most from them.

The language barriers faced by families for whom English is a second language may lead to delays in their receiving diagnoses and associated services. Immigrant families may not consider the possibility that the library has free programs for them. The parents of autistic children in low-income families may not have the resources for expensive early interventions, or understand how to access them. And Black autistic children are more likely than white children to be misdiagnosed initially, potentially causing them to miss out on critical early services.[6] It is important that all families know that your library has programs and resources available to help them, especially those who may be at risk of less access to services elsewhere. Offering inclusive library programs and services, as well as information about other community resources, can help these families to bridge the access gaps they may encounter.

We should note here that it is important to create programming that is *relevant* for varied demographic groups. It is not enough to simply invite children and families if the programming is not designed for their needs and the materials don't reflect their experiences. For example, if you bring in children who primarily speak Spanish, you should incorporate Spanish-language materials into your storytime. Or even better, have a bilingual storyteller.

Think of creative ways you can communicate the library's commitment to inclusive services to these community members. Make personal connections, and invite these families to your programs whenever you see them in the library. Reach out beyond the library, too, and provide program information to the community organizations in your area.

AUTISM, LIBRARIES, AND INTERSECTIONALITY
Adriana White

It is important that librarians consider the intersectional identities of their autistic patrons. Every autistic patron we serve has a distinctly different life experience, depending on factors such as their race, gender, class, and more.

Understanding Intersectionality

According to Professor Kimberlé Crenshaw's theory of intersectionality, when we want to talk about protected categories—like disability, race, or gender —we cannot focus solely on single issues. As Audre Lorde famously wrote, "there is no such thing as a single-issue struggle because we do not live single-issue lives." For example, Black, Indigenous, or people of color (often abbreviated to BIPOC) who happen to be disabled have noted that it is impossible to view them as solely BIPOC or solely disabled—one trait cannot be viewed without taking into account the influence of the other. Disabled BIPOC face social isolation, accusations of laziness, and misinterpretations of their unconventional behaviors. These intersectional groups encounter bias and microaggressions in several facets of their everyday lives, beyond what their peers face.

The patrons we serve in our libraries are diverse, and their overlapping identities will require different actions from us. It is our responsibility to notice and acknowledge the complexities of these identities, so we can create libraries that serve the needs of our diverse communities.

Libraries and Intersectional Autism

The two main ideas we should take away from the concept of intersectionality are (1) diversity exists (even when we don't see it), and (2) diversity matters (even when we think it doesn't).

While most media representations of autism tend to be white, young, heterosexual males, the reality of autism is much more diverse. Diagnosis rates for Latinx children lag far behind the diagnosis rates of white and Black children, and Black and Latinx children are often diagnosed much later than their white counterparts. Girls also tend to be diagnosed later than boys. Many Latinx autistic adults, myself included, were not diagnosed until adulthood, because we were too similar to other odd family members, or our behaviors were misinterpreted and misattributed to other conditions (such as anxiety or just plain disobedience).

What this means for libraries is that while we may have some patrons who are explicitly autistic, there will also be autistic patrons whose autism will be harder to spot. By assuming diversity in our autism planning, we can meet the needs of additional autistic patrons, without requiring them to explicitly disclose their autism to us.

We must also assume diversity because we cannot create truly accessible spaces without considering intersectionality. Accommodations that we create with one category of patron in mind may not work for patrons in other marginalized groups. For example, large-print signage for patrons with vision impairments may need to be printed in multiple languages, and sign-language interpreters may need to be located against a plain backdrop for patrons with sensory-processing sensitivities.

It is especially important to consider the intersection of race and autism. Since the rise of the Black Lives Matter movement, autistic self-advocates and parents of autistic children have raised concerns about interactions between Black autistics and the police. A person who is autistic, or deaf, or disabled in some other way may not respond appropriately to commands from law enforcement, which has the potential to lead to dangerous misunderstandings.

As a result of this, Black autistics and parents of Black autistic children may feel uncomfortable with library initiatives that include the presence of police officers. While a storytime event with a police officer may fall under the seemingly uncontroversial umbrella of "community helpers" (a common unit in special education classrooms), libraries may discover that their Black families are not interested in attending such an event.

This revelation may come as a surprise to some librarians, especially since the neutrality of libraries is considered a core characteristic of the field. While libraries are often thought of as neutral spaces, the reality is much more complicated. Every action we take, from the books we purchase to the programs we create, is an intentional choice, and an extension of our vision and mission. If we declare our libraries to be dedicated to diversity and inclusivity, then we may find that neutrality can conflict with those principles.

When faced with the choice between neutrality and inclusivity, libraries should make a conscious effort to focus on being safe spaces for marginalized groups. Simply put, a library that favors neutrality over diversity will not be considered a safe option for many library patrons. When a choice is made to include groups that advocate for the oppression of others, libraries are likely to find that many of their patrons will choose to stay away.

While topics like intersectionality and neutrality are indeed complex and perhaps a bit overwhelming, it is no reason to avoid the conversation. Libraries should not throw up their hands and give up! Rather, this should be viewed as a call for libraries to engage in meaningful dialogue and partnerships with the many diverse groups within their communities. We can make space for our diverse patrons, invite them to co-create library spaces and programming, and allow their needs to guide our efforts. By reaching out to diverse patrons, and the community organizations that serve them, we gain another set of eyes through which we can see our libraries. These fresh perspectives can help make our libraries better. See "Appendix B: Recommended Resources for Intersectional Practice."

Wording in Promotional Materials

It's only natural that you will want to be respectful when planning and implementing autism programming, and you will want to use language that reflects that mindset. But what is the right language to use when referring to autistic people? This is a hot-button topic, and one that will probably continue to shift and evolve as more conversations take place. We touched on this a bit in the introduction and chapter 1, but a more robust discussion is necessary as you begin to think about planning and promoting your programs.

Though many autistic adults advocate the use of identity-first language, the parents of autistic children may feel differently. "Autistic" may still feel offensive to them, as if you are calling their child or teen a bad word or using a negative slur. While this is far from the case, we suggest that you use the language that makes your community feel the most comfortable. Are you working with a community group that describes their members as "having autism"? Or are you inviting in a group of teens who describe themselves as "autistic," or who refer to themselves as "Autistics"? Take your cues from the community members you are working with, and meet them where they are.

If you are still uncomfortable with person-first vs. identity-first language, try using more general inclusive language. This is a wonderful approach, as some children and teens might not have a diagnosis yet, but their families know they would benefit from more support. Here is an example of how the Henrico County (VA) Public Library, has met this challenge: "Sensory Storytime engages children through movement, music, stories, sensory activities, and play. This welcoming, encouraging, and supportive program is smaller and more adaptive than other storytimes. An early intervention professional will assist."

Budget and Funding

Cost always plays a big part in planning library programs. Some of the programs presented in this book use costly equipment and software, and such programs are often funded by grants. If you are thinking about applying for a grant, look to organizations or groups that support programs for children with disabilities, as well as those that provide grants to libraries. The "Autism Welcome Here" grant, funded by Barbara Klipper and sponsored by Libraries and Autism: We're Connected, offers a total of $5,000 every year to fund one or more initiatives in libraries in the United States and Canada. Grant proposals must be for programs or services that directly or indirectly benefit autistic people or their families. Several other possibilities are listed in "Appendix D: Funding Sources."

Grants are not the only solution. Look into the organizations in your community that serve autistic children and their families. They may be able to provide funds or donate materials or equipment.

If you do find yourself at a dead end with fundraising, you can still implement most of the programs in this book with a minimal outlay of cash, as long as you add a dose of ingenuity and creativity. We have suggested less expensive alternatives whenever possible, and include links to printables when applicable. We have also included books and websites that suggest inexpensive sensory-based activities in "Appendix E: Sensory Integration Activities." It is also part of inclusion to work to have these programs become part of the regular library budget.

Scheduling

Young autistic children are often heavily scheduled with other services and community programs, and they may not be able to attend storytimes if you offer them on weekday mornings. You may get more participation from those families if you schedule your programs on weekends. On the other hand, teens, who are often less involved than their peers in after-school sports and social activities, may really appreciate after-school or evening programs that give them something to do and an opportunity to meet and engage with friends. As with many of these considerations, you should survey your community members to determine the times that work best for them.

In addition to determining the times to schedule your programs, you will also have to decide on their frequency. Series allow a more cohesive group to form, and the participants can practice and develop their skills over a period of time. On the other hand, if you have limited staff and resources, you might prefer to offer a monthly program rather than one or two series, so that more people can attend and so that programs are available throughout the year.

Whatever you decide to do in terms of scheduling, bear in mind that autistic people prefer routine and predictability, so it is preferable to maintain the same schedule for your program over time.

Collaboration

As someone who might not be an expert in autism or special education, you may be nervous about working with these children or teens on your own. You might wonder if you know what to do, or what to say. First, let us assure you that you'll be just fine. And you should know that you don't have to be totally on your own. Let the entire staff of the library know that you are creating programs for autistic young people. Given today's increased awareness and understanding of autism, it is not a stretch to imagine that someone on your staff might be able to contribute from personal experience. You can also reach out into your community for partners.

COLLABORATION WITH COMMUNITY MEMBERS
Hope Hill Clark

Programming for children on the autism spectrum provides an opportunity to collaborate with other community members and expand the library's resources in doing so. There are nonprofit organizations, disability-focused organizations, child development centers, local businesses, parent support groups, and speech and occupational therapists in the private sector with whom we can develop collaborative partnerships. In doing so, we can promote the library as a valuable meeting space and resource where all of its patrons can feel at ease. Families with autistic children want the library to be a space that includes all of their children, with or without a disability.

Partnerships with other types of entities have also resulted in successful programs, and there are likely opportunities in your community. For example, there may be a symphony orchestra or movie theater in your area that offers sensory-friendly events. You can explore if these organizations would partner with you on a program for autistic children and teens.

Our biggest recommendation for collaboration is to involve autistic self-advocates. Though you will be planning programs for children and teens, young adults and adults who are autistic will be your best resource—they were once children themselves, and can provide feedback based on their own experiences.

NOTHING ABOUT US, WITHOUT US: CENTERING AUTISTICS IN THE CONVERSATION
"Justin Spectrum"

Nihil de nobis, sine nobis. "Nothing about us, without us." This concept has existed for centuries across various social movements. For more than two decades it has been associated with disability rights. James Charlton wrote of hearing the slogan in 1993 from two South African activists who had themselves picked it up at an international disability rights conference in Europe.[7]

An awareness of those five words ("nothing about us, without us") are crucial to be able to best serve Autistic children and teens in your library. Perhaps you have watched a presentation by a mental health professional describing the symptoms of autism, or watched a fellow library worker demonstrate a "sensory storytime" meant to be more comforting to an Autistic child. This knowledge is not inherently a bad thing, but it should not be forgotten that the truest experts on autism are Autistic people. To learn more about how to best serve Autistic people, ask us, or read what we write!

Library workers should develop a basic understanding of disability rights and disability studies and the Autistic self-advocacy movement. A "disability studies lens" makes it easier for any person to accept Autistic people, and to avoid viewing autism as a problem to be solved. Seeing the barriers that are socially constructed around autistic people are helpful, both to accommodating kids and teens in your library as well as to working positively with Autistic adults (whether they be your patrons or your coworkers).

Evaluation

Earlier in this chapter, we explored goals you might set for your programs. Throughout the design and implementation of your program, it's important to evaluate the program to understand if it is meeting those goals. And if it is not, it's time to adjust. As librarian Kate Thompson says: "Feedback is critical both in design and post-program when you are serving a specific audience. Too often I hear that people want to do programs but struggle with low attendance, and I think forming an (online) committee of caregivers or at least doing frequent surveys of your patrons can really help identify what the barriers are and make your programs more specific and useful."

PROGRAM EVALUATION   *Reina Malakoff*

Programs can be evaluated in many ways besides tallying the number of participants. The value of a program might be measured by the testimonials of those who attend; an easy check-off exit ticket or a message board describing patrons' experiences with a program might illustrate its importance. A program might be part of a bigger plan to establish comfort for a community that is underserved. Kowalsky and Woodruff echo this idea, noting that "when members of such underserved groups have positive experiences, it may result in lifelong reconnections with a library."[8]

Furthermore, a program might be evaluated by the connections it fosters with individuals and organizations. Collaborating with people or organizations representing underserved populations can help librarians gain experience and understand certain populations. This empowers patrons, staff, and organizations alike to provide an important comprehensive community. According to Flaherty, "as public library staff move beyond the walls of the library to extend beyond traditional roles and provide more varied services, it will become more necessary than ever to develop cooperative relationships with community partners."[9]

Final Thoughts

Are you all set with your planning decisions? Maybe not, but you should know enough by now to get started. If you have questions about anything, from inclusion to scheduling, remember that you can always turn to autism parents, professionals, and self-advocates in your community for help.

NOTES

1. Center for Universal Design, "The Principles of Universal Design, Version 2.0," North Carolina State University, 1997, https://projects.ncsu.edu/ncsu/design/cud/about_ud/udprinciplestext.htm.

2. CAST, "Universal Design for Learning Guidelines, Version 2.2," 2018, http://udlguidelines.cast.org.

3. American Library Association, "Library Bill of Rights," June 30, 2006, http://www.ala.org/advocacy/intfreedom/librarybill.

4. Amelia Anderson, "Autism and the Academic Library: A Study of Online Communication," *College & Research Libraries* 79, no. 5 (2018): 645.

5. Anderson, "Autism and the Academic Library," 645.

6. David Mandell, Richard F. Ittenbach, Susan E. Levy, and Jennifer A. Pinto-Martin, "Disparities in Diagnoses Received Prior to a Diagnosis of Autism Spectrum Disorder," *Journal of Autism and Developmental Disorders* 37, no. 9 (2007): 1795–1802.

7. James I. Charlton, *Nothing About Us Without Us: Disability Oppression and Empowerment* (Berkeley: University of California Press, 2000), 3.

8. Michelle Kowalsky and John Woodruff, *Creating Inclusive Library Environments: A Planning Guide for Serving Patrons with Disabilities* (Chicago: American Library Association, 2016), 111.

9. Mary Grace Flaherty, *Promoting Individual and Community Health at the Library* (Chicago: American Library Association, 2018), 91.

Best Practices

ONCE YOU HAVE COMPLETED THE PRELIMINARY PLANNING FOR YOUR program, the next thing to do is to understand best practices. These practices will support your autistic patrons, both in inclusive groups and in programs designed just for them. In formulating your dream program, you may find that you cannot incorporate everything you would like to do. As always, the realities of budget, staffing, and available space may limit your plans. Don't give up. It is better to offer a program that doesn't include every desirable element than not do a program at all. If you started by introducing universal design principles, as introduced in chapter 2, you have already set the stage for success. Then you can integrate the following simple suggestions for creating successful inclusive programs:

1. Limit enrollment.
2. Have teen or adult assistants.
3. Prepare the participants for the program.
4. Use visual supports.
5. Manage transitions.
6. Control the environment.
7. Provide seating options.
8. Supply fidgets and other sensory tools.
9. Designate quiet or sensory rooms.
10. Incorporate repetition and routine.
11. Provide structure while being flexible and understanding.

Each of these elements will be discussed in detail in the sections below.

Limit Enrollment

Because no two autistic people are alike, small groups make it easier to customize a program to meet the needs of the participants and to provide individual support as needed. A smaller group also means fewer opportunities for distraction. Many librarians restrict the size of their programs for autistic children to around eight to ten children and their caregivers. In inclusive programs, you may find it more of a challenge to limit enrollment, particularly for popular events or presenters. In these cases we suggest having assistants, as described next.

Have Teen or Adult Assistants

As a general rule, it is difficult for one librarian working alone to conduct a program. The components of the program itself will determine the number of adults you will need. You may want to have two leaders or one leader and an assistant, such as a library page or volunteer. You may also consider getting additional support by asking parents to assist you in working with their children, even if parents of children that age don't normally stay in the program room. Parents can give you a few extra pairs of hands, they can be helpful in managing stressful situations, and they can work one-on-one with their own children in performing the program's activities.

For programs geared toward older children or teens, you may not need to have parents present. Teens in particular will probably prefer this. Are you nervous about having the parents leave? Ask them to stay nearby the first time or two until you have a better idea of how each child acts in the group.

Prepare Participants for the Program

New situations can be intimidating for anyone. If your library or program is new to them, an autistic child or teen may be so uncomfortable that they won't be open to enjoying the experience. You can mitigate this anxiety by doing a few simple things to prepare them for the program in advance. This is known as "priming."

Library Tours and Open Houses

One technique used in priming is the open house or library tour. Can you let families come for a first visit before the library opens to the public, or after it closes for the evening? This will give children and teens a sense of what to expect when they come back, even when there are more distractions present. Even if you can't do this, a tour during open hours is a great idea. The Deerfield (IL) Public Library has used this method, hosting an open house on the Wednesday before a Saturday program in order to familiarize the registrants with the space and the program content.

Virtual Tours

You should also consider recording a video or virtual tour of the library. Children and their caregivers can watch this tour from home as many times as they need to prepare for a library visit in person. This is something that will be helpful for all children, and especially those who are autistic. Be sure to feature every space, in order, that a child will encounter when coming to visit the library. This includes the front door of the public library, all the way through to your children's room. And don't forget the restrooms and water fountains! Check out an excellent example online from the Washington-Centerville Public Library, or search "public library virtual tours" for more current examples.[1]

Social Stories

Another way to prime children for programs or visits is to provide a Social Story in advance. The Social Story concept was developed by Carol Gray in 1991 and was later modified by others. *Social Stories* are used to help autistic children better understand the nuances of interpersonal communication so that they can interact with others in an effective and appropriate way. Each Social Story describes a social situation that the child may encounter. The story includes the important social cues of that situation and the behaviors that will be expected. Sometimes photos or other images are used in conjunction with a Social Story, so the child can more concretely visualize where the event will take place. You might create a general Social Story for visiting the library, or a more specific one to prepare the registrants of a particular program. These are only helpful if the child has time to read them in advance, so think of how to facilitate this. For programs, perhaps you could e-mail a Social Story to all participants who register in advance. For a general "visiting the library" Social Story, you could post it online. For a good example of how to do this, see the Social Story posted online from the Deerfield Public Library.[2]

Use Visual Supports

When images are used as a communication tool, they are known as "visual supports," and libraries have used them in many different ways. Visual supports can be created from photographs, pictures you draw, or they can be ones that you create using specialized software. In general, the more realistic the representations are, the better they will be understood. Boardmaker, published by Mayer-Johnson, is the most commonly used software for this purpose, although it can be expensive. Before you buy any programs, however, talk to a customer service representative to make sure the software will give you at least some of the images and capabilities you need for your library program. You might ask if there is a free trial you could explore before purchase, or other less expensive options that will serve the same purpose.

Visual Schedules

A visual schedule is used to help make a program predictable. Visual schedules can be designed in a variety of ways. The most common is to create a visual of each program element as a separate rectangle or square, laminate it, and attach it to a poster board with a Velcro strip. The images can be small or large. You can remove each picture from the board as the activity is completed, or leave them all up throughout the program. This board should be highly visible throughout the program, and you should refer to it as you transition between program elements.

FIGURE 3.1 Visual schedule

Visual schedule based on one used during a Sensory Storytime at the Ferguson Library

Supports for Older Children and Teens

While a visual schedule works well for all storytimes, it might feel too "young" to older kids and teens. However, these patrons will still benefit from having information presented visually about the program they are attending. Try creating a handout that kids and teens can pick up when they walk into the room that clearly illustrates what will happen in your library program, and in what order. This organizational tool will be helpful for anyone in attendance, so think about incorporating it into all of your inclusive programs.

Manage Transitions

The autistic children and teens you work with might need support as they transition from one activity to another during a program. You can use your visual schedule to help children transition by pointing out the next image as each activity ends, or by removing the images on the board as activities are completed. If your program includes crafts or other activities that are open-ended and take place away from the activity schedule, you can help children navigate the transition with verbal or visual reminders of the elapsed time and a warning of how much time remains for the activity.

There are a number of inexpensive timers you can use so that program participants can keep track of elapsed time themselves. One example is called a visual timer, and these can be easily purchased online. Although these timers may be useful tools to have, they aren't necessary. It's fine for you to just keep track of the time yourself. Be sure to announce when the children have five more minutes of the activity remaining and again one minute before the activity is to end. Abrupt changes when a child is deeply engrossed in an activity can precipitate a meltdown in some children, and transition warnings can prevent this from happening. Any sound can alert children that it is time to transition to the next activity as long as it is not too loud and jarring. Singing, using a chime, or tapping a drum can all work. To help young children transition from one area of the room to another, try having them move in a special and fun way. Try flying like a bird or an airplane, or trotting like a horse. One librarian blows bubbles to get the children's attention and then direct them to the next area. Others use their hands to make the American Sign Language (ASL) sign for "finished" to indicate that an activity is over. It's an easy sign to learn. Start with your palms facing your chest, then move them away from your body and turn them quickly so your palms end up facing the children.

You should provide information to children and caregivers about program timing and what they can expect with each transition. You might post this online. For example, "For the first 30 minutes of our program we will read and sing. Then, for the next 30 minutes we will have sensory play time." The more detail you can provide, the better your attendees will be prepared for transitions during the program.

Control the Environment

There are two main reasons to control the environment when creating programming for autistic children and teens. The first reason is to minimize negative sensory input. The second is to add predictability, which makes many autistic people feel more comfortable.

Ideally, you would be able to provide a completely safe and distraction-free program space that looks the same way for every program. But in the real world, this is rarely possible. Even if your program room is multipurpose and full of stuff, there are a number of things you can do to make the space more autism-friendly. In controlling the environment to benefit your autistic youth, you will find that these modifications make the environment more universally accessible for all.

Try some or all of these approaches:

- Reduce distracting noises or sounds. Autistic people who also have some type of sensory processing disorder (SPD) may have a strong aversion to certain smells, textures, or sounds. Moreover, because autistic people may be unable to filter out ambient sensory input, sounds like a running vacuum cleaner in the next room can be distracting.
- Offer the participants options to reduce sensory input when an environmental situation is out of your control. As librarian Renee Grassi says, "The night before [an autism open house] there was a chili bakeoff. The whole room smelled! You can't control this. We'd already launched accessibility kits and they had nose plugs. I kept this out as an option, and one of the individuals came in and was offended by the smell and I showed him this. You can't always control the space, but you can provide supports for people to manage and mitigate their experiences."
- Avoid fluorescent lighting if at all possible. Many autistic people can see these lights flicker or hear them buzzing, and they find them very disturbing. If you do have fluorescent light fixtures, make sure the bulbs are new. Or you can use classroom light filters, which have been reported to calm adults as well as children. If you have fluorescent lighting that can't be covered, you can provide light-filtering options like cheap sunglasses and baseball caps. Librarian Kate Thompson suggests installing a dimmer switch for lights, which makes the space even more adaptable, and is a great solution for programs such as sensory-friendly movies. If the lighting can't be changed, Thompson recommends using a few table lamps instead of overhead lighting, which creates a homey atmosphere.
- Eliminate drafts from down-blowing vents by covering the vents or redirecting the airflow.
- Keep the room as empty of clutter and distractions as possible. Visible items in the room can be distracting to the point where children aren't able to focus on the program activities. Store materials in bins or cabinets if you can, or cover them with sheets. As with programming for any group of children, you'll want to remove books from lower shelves where children can grab them, and block off areas that have potentially dangerous items.
- Have a designated area where visual supports can be placed during programs, and orient that room the same way each time. A large flannel board or bulletin board can be used for your visuals. You can also buy a large trifold, portable tabletop display. These can be pretty expensive, but they are sturdy and can help to designate the front of the room. Or you can simply DIY by tacking up a large piece of felt onto a frame, a wall, or a bulletin board.
- Set up a quiet corner where children can retreat from the program without leaving the room. If possible, try to keep this area free from distractions.

- If at all possible, have a sink in the room or provide wet wipes or paper towels. Some autistic kids are tactilely defensive and will want to wash their hands immediately after using craft materials.
- Leave room in the back for children who need to get up to pace or stim during the program.
- Take a picture of the room after you set it up for the first program. This will help you prepare a similar environment the next time the group gets together, adding to its predictability.

Provide Seating Options

Have seating that supports children, helps them focus, and delineates personal space. Provide multiple options so children and teens can choose the type of seat that works best for their individual needs. Some options include the following:

- Educubes, also called cube chairs, are brightly colored, sturdy plastic cubes that offer flexible seating for young children. Their prices vary, so shop around online.
- HowdaHug seats, which are especially designed as seating for autistic children, are folding and slatted chairs that sit directly on the floor. Children are held snugly, and they can rock while seated. HowdaHugs can store easily, but they are costly.
- BackJack chairs are essentially padded cushions attached to a back, allowing people to sit comfortably on the floor and have back support. BackJacks are generally less expensive than Educubes or HowdaHugs and are easy to stack and store.
- Rocking Bowls are big enough for small children to sit inside, and rock around in.
- Tactile air cushions provide individual seating on the floor and sensory input. You can find relatively inexpensive disc or balance cushions easily through an online search.
- Wobble stools allow children and teens to rock and wiggle while still planted firmly on the ground.
- Carpet squares, small mats, and cushions are inexpensive, low-tech seating options that you can purchase, or may already have. Allow children to pick their favorite carpet square to use; using the same color square at every library program will give them a sense of security through a predictable routine.
- The least expensive option is to use colored tape on the floor to designate seating and set apart areas for different activities. Remember that anything that visually defines where they are supposed to be in space will help children better understand personal boundaries and behavioral expectations.

Don't forget to also have seating available that works for adult caregivers. Portable stools that can be arranged behind the children's seating work well.

Supply Fidgets and Other Sensory Tools

It is a good idea to keep a box of squeeze balls and other small handheld items that kids or teens can manipulate while waiting or during the program. In the autism world these are known as fidgets or fidget toys. If you've ever clicked a pen, twirled your hair, or rubbed a stone when anxious, you have an idea of what it is like when an autistic person uses a fidget. You might even be familiar with the fidget spinner craze from a few years back. These types of toys truly do serve a purpose. Rather than getting upset if a child or teen seems to spend more attention on manipulating a toy than on your program, remember that this actually helps them to focus their attention. It is likely that some of your children and teens will come with one of their favorite fidgets already in hand or pocket. You should also provide a selection of fidgets for children and teens in your programs, and have these readily available in an obvious spot in the room. Let attendees know that they are there and are meant to be used. You can find inexpensive items in toy and dollar stores, such as chenille sticks (pipe cleaners), rubber bands, and soft squeeze balls.

A creative way you can use fidgets is to indicate whose turn it is to speak during a book discussion or other program for older children. Using a fidget as a turn-taking object serves two purposes: it lets everyone know clearly and concretely if they are supposed to talk, and it gives the speaker something to fidget with while speaking in front of the group, thereby reducing their anxiety.

Offer Sensory Kits

Try supplying fidgets and more with a sensory kit that is available for patrons to use when they come in the library. In an effort to support all patrons, the Deerfield Public Library's youth services librarian, Julia Frederick, and the adult services outreach associate, Vicki Karlovsky, created sensory kits to have at the front information desk, the youth services desk, and the adult services desk. These kits are meant to help patrons of all abilities have a more enjoyable time in the library.

Each kit contains six different fidgets (tangles, stretchy string fidgets, etc.), a pair of noise-canceling headphones, a mirror, and two emotions sheets (one with pictures of adults and one with pictures of children). As Frederick says, "We hope that patrons feel free to use whatever they need—there is no need to ask for them at the desk, but we do ask that patrons return the item(s) when they are finished with them."

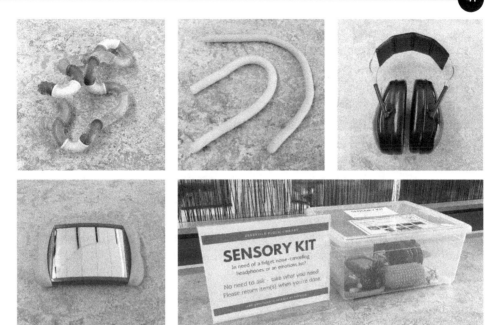

FIGURE 3.2 Sensory kit items

Example sensory kit and sensory kit items at the Deerfield Public Library

Designate Sensory or Quiet Rooms

Some libraries are able to provide more than just a quiet corner in their program room. If you have the available space, consider designating an unused study room, meeting room, or office as a quiet room. Or take the idea a step further and create a sensory room, like the Sensory Strategy Space at the Louisville (OH) Public Library. This space is divided into two sections; one provides sensory interaction opportunities, and the other is a relaxation area.

QUIET ROOMS AND SPACES *Kate Thompson*

If your library has a nursing room, consider making it a flexible space by keeping the decor neutral. Since many autistic people have sensory sensitivities, leave the changing tables and diaper pail in the bathroom, rather than the nursing room. If you include a sink, avoid using an electric hand dryer. This rooms functions as a space for prayer as well.

If your library has study rooms, consider dedicating one as a "quiet space" where you will provide adjustable lighting, comfortable seating, and fidget items. Truly soundproof spaces are ideal but hard to find, so consider providing a white noise machine.

Include your program room in the Social Story you create for your library. Use photographs of the room or the quiet corner, and include text indicating that this is a space where patrons can go if they need to take a break. Including the space in the Social Story gives patrons a chance to get comfortable with the idea before they even enter your program.

Be sure to announce the availability of quiet spaces at the start of every program, letting patrons know there is a quiet space available and where it is. This extends not just to programs designed for a specific audience, but to all programs you provide. Let patrons know that they may leave at any time, and are welcome to return to the program without being concerned that they are interrupting it. By letting patrons know about the availability of these spaces and your behavior expectations, you're also indicating that you're aware of the needs of various families, and that they are welcome at your programs. The welcoming attitude of staff is as important in creating a friendly atmosphere as the physical space.

Incorporate Repetition and Routine

In a world of unpredictable outcomes, many autistic people have a strong desire for sameness. They might like reading the same book, listening to the same song, or doing the same activity multiple times. Repetition allows them to build skills, and routine and repetition make a program predictable, which lessens their anxiety. Having many elements that repeat each time the program is offered is one way to introduce repetition; using books with repetitive elements is another. Setting the program room up the same way each time, following the same sequence of events, and using the same greetings and goodbye activities are additional ways to build in routine.

Routine does not have to mean boring. Routines give children something to look forward to, and something to plan for. Children can look forward to singing their favorite song, or reading along with a well-loved book. Routines help to provide structure and familiarity, and relieve stress over the unknown. Most importantly, routines help to ensure that autistic children and teens have a positive experience in your library.

Provide Structure while Being Flexible and Understanding

The characteristics of autism manifest differently in every person, and even having a good understanding of the disorder might not prepare you for all of the situations you'll encounter. You should allow for program attendees to fidget and stim, and make sure they are all aware that these behaviors are not just acceptable but encouraged. Be generous and flexible whenever possible. This doesn't mean you should allow behavior that ruins the program for others. It is okay to tell a parent that their child is disrupting the program to the point where they will need to leave for a while. Do this in a kindly way, and provide a place in the library where they can go for a while to regroup. If they are able to join the program once more, on that day or another time, be sure to welcome them back.

EVENT MANAGEMENT *Karen Stoll Farrell*

Sometimes we attend library events, even though we know that they will be difficult. As an Autistic family, each of us has an individual limit for how much noise, people, and general input we can handle, but many of us also enjoy going out to public events sometimes, as well. Library and outdoor public events are often more accessible for us than some others. In attending these, I have found that there are key differences that make an event more successful for us.

Events that allow us to leave and come back at a moment's notice without worrying about asking permission or explaining ourselves to someone are critical. Someone in our family is likely to need a quick break during the event, and we will need to find somewhere quiet or need to access the outdoors at a moment's notice. We might even need to leave the event entirely, but perhaps with the hope that we can come back a bit later.

My husband and I look for events that give a lot of information in advance: we prefer to access maps of the building, timing of events, descriptions of crafts, or even explanations of how wait times for popular events will be handled. All of this eases our own anxieties, allows us to plan and structure the day, and enables our children to know what to expect. When there are less unexpected occurrences, everyone is better able to handle the additional sensory stressors that a crowded event can bring.

A couple of things help us at the event itself: a setup that is truly accessible, with wide paths between tables, is very important. My son, in particular, has a very difficult time managing people crowding him constantly. Sometimes this is inescapable, but any mitigation is useful, including spacing out chairs at craft tables, creating "one way" signs for particularly narrow walking areas, and cordoning off sections so that people walking are not crowding and bumping those seated at a table.

While our children have learned about navigating lines, we occasionally find an event that places 'X's of tape on the floor for kids to stand on. We have found that this helps with crowding and space issues. On the other hand, some events don't require lines at all and instead keep a list of names and times for children to return. This is even more preferable for long waits, with one caveat: if the timing is different from what they are told to expect, our kids will find this more stressful. Once they waited for a turn at a virtual reality game with a teenaged volunteer who was not closely monitoring the time. My son got quite frustrated, but solved it by timing the turns himself and letting the volunteer know when he thought their turn should be over.

44

Offering written instructions and visuals for crafts is also helpful. One of our daughters often becomes confused and distressed by verbal instructions. She much prefers to grab an instruction sheet, a handful of supplies, and sort it out independently. If she is able to get to the crafts without being required to ask someone that is even better.

Relatedly, we all feel much better when people don't take it personally that she won't speak to them, or when our other daughter's voice is too loud, or when our son tells them the best way for everyone to take fair turns. The most important sign of success for us at events is not whether people have considered every accommodation, but whether people are able to be flexible and understanding of our family's different needs.

Final Thoughts

The suggestions in this chapter are what you need to start planning programs that will be more inclusive of autistic children and teens. The rest of this book explores specific program ideas for different age groups, school libraries, and families. You'll find that the tips in this chapter can be integrated into whatever program you plan.

NOTES

1. Washington-Centerville Public Library, "Children's Library Tour," www.youtube.com/watch?v=HSOB2BLEZn4.

2. Deerfield Public Library, "Youth Social Story," https://deerfieldlibrary.org/youth-social-story.

Storytime Programs for Young Children

STORYTIMES FORM THE BACKBONE OF PROGRAMMING FOR YOUNG children in most public libraries and many school libraries, offering our youngest patrons the opportunity to learn through songs, books, rhymes, and movement.

Storytimes are more than just fun and games—they play an important role in early childhood education. A large-scale study showed that children attending public library storytimes exhibited many types of early literacy behaviors.[1] Making connections through words and songs helps young children lay the foundation for a lifetime of learning. Establishing these connections in a fun, social environment also helps children associate stories with enjoyment, which often fosters a lifelong love of reading.

And storytimes aren't just for the benefit of children. By modeling interactive and engaging reading strategies, fingerplays, and songs, librarians are also playing the role of "media mentors" for parents and caregivers, providing them with ideas to replicate at home. One study found that the gaps in school readiness skills between high- and low-income households have declined steadily. Many factors likely play a role in this gap, but the authors partially attribute the trend to "changes in parenting practices that have increased low-income children's exposure to cognitively stimulating activities at home."[2] Every Child Ready to Read @ your library (ECRR) and similar parent education initiatives have probably been contributing factors here. ECRR describes five practices that make a difference in early literacy development: talking, singing, reading, writing, and playing, and these practices are frequently introduced in storytimes.[3] In providing free services for all members of their communities, librarians have played a role in promoting and modeling these learning activities for low-income families and other groups who might not have access to such enrichment elsewhere.

All young children benefit from participating in an information-rich storytime environment, and autistic children and their families benefit perhaps to an even greater extent. When engaging in a supportive storytime program, autistic children can interact with and learn alongside their peers, something that will benefit them when they begin school. Parents and caregivers can find community by connecting with other welcoming families.

Before we provide you with ideas for storytimes that you can replicate, this chapter will give you some foundational information. We'll cover the types of storytimes you might plan, general tips for including autistic children, and finally some ideas for choosing books and music for your programs.

Types of Storytimes

Libraries typically take a number of different approaches with their storytimes for autistic children, including inclusive storytimes, storytimes designed specifically for autistic children, and sensory storytimes.

Inclusive Storytimes

Inclusive storytimes typically include both autistic and neurotypical children. They resemble a typical library storytime in many ways, and consist of the usual combination of books, flannel board stories, fingerplays, and movement activities. Sometimes they include a craft or art project. What distinguishes these storytimes from more traditional library programs is their application of some of the best practices for use with autistic children; for example, they may use visual supports, limit the group's size, have designated seating, and control the environment in other ways. They often include sensory integration activities. These approaches allow all children to participate, no matter their abilities.

Storytimes Designed Specifically for Autistic Children

Some libraries also refer to these as supported, or adapted, programs. These storytimes are typically limited to a small group of children and their parents or caregivers, and advance registration is usually required. Because these storytimes aim to solely meet the needs of autistic children, they utilize many of the best practices as described earlier in this book.

Because inclusion is so important for all children, this approach might seem problematic at first glance. However, these programs are highly valued by many families. Some families appreciate the opportunity to gather with other children and parents with whom they uniquely relate and with whom they can share experiences. They prefer an environment that assures them their children will be understood by all others in attendance. This is understandable, given that many parents of autistic kids have experienced holding their breath in fear that their child will be disruptive and they'll have to leave a situation. While all libraries should strive for acceptance in all situations, sometimes we fall short of establishing a climate of welcome and respect for everyone as they are in our programs. With a targeted program, these families can relax, knowing the program leader or another attendee won't say something or look askance at their children. Targeted programs can also be a bridge to inclusive programs. Some children start with them, get comfortable, and are then able to participate successfully in inclusive settings with more sensory input and participants. Others are never able to make that transition. All of these are reasons why both types of programs have value.

Sensory Storytimes

A sensory storytime is a public library storytime program that is especially well-suited for autistic children. A sensory storytime generally follows a unique program model and is designed for children with sensory sensitivities. The emphasis is often on sensory integration activities, although books, movement, and rhymes may also be part of the mix. A sensory storytime can be a welcome addition to a storytime roster, one that librarians will enjoy doing and patrons both with and without sensory sensitivities will enjoy attending. Sensory storytimes can be conducted as either inclusive or autism-specific programs.

Librarian Jen Taggart, who blogs at *Adaptive Umbrella*, says that her sensory storytimes have been much more successful since she added what she describes as "multisensory experiences" while reading stories. As she says: "When you think of sensory storytime, you think of visual schedules, and stories, and activities where you're using sensory tools. I'm incorporating all of that, but I'm also incorporating multisensory experiences when I read stories. For example, if we're reading a picture book about gardening, I'll bring in plants for kids to touch and smell. It gives a lot more meaning to the story when the kids experience that multisensory element."

If you intend to do a sensory storytime, it is important to understand what this program is and is not. It is not an opportunity for sensory bombardment or offering a wide range of sensory opportunities. Providing children with things to smell, touch, and taste is good, but doing so does not constitute a sensory storytime. Many librarians are confused and misinformed on this point. The sensory activities integrated into a sensory storytime serve a specific purpose, addressing one or more sensory-based issues that are common in these children. And because children can be either sensory seekers or sensory avoiders, it is essential that sensory storytimes, as well as sensory rooms, offer activities and materials that serve both groups. Refer back to chapter 1 for a general description of sensory processing disorders (SPDs) and their relation to autism. You can also easily find out more, as well as activities to add to your programs, by searching online for "sensory integration activities."

Experiment with Your Storytime Programs

You can spend some time experimenting with variations on these storytime programs to determine which approach best meets your community's needs. Some autistic children will find an inclusive storytime to still be too overwhelming, while others will thrive on it. Or, you might find that your sensory storytimes attract a much wider audience than just your autism families. You can always provide multiple options for your families if you have the staffing to do so. This is an example of Universal Design for Learning in action. Whatever approach you find to be the most successful, participation in one or more of these storytime programs will help autistic children build early literacy skills and form the positive foundation for a lifetime of learning and library use.

Try Backward Chaining

If you aren't able to offer any of these programs in your library, or if you have a family who wants to bring their child to a traditional storytime and you're not sure if the child will be able to participate successfully, you can try a technique called "backward chaining." Instead of having the child come at the beginning, when things may be chaotic, and risking them having to leave in the middle, start them out by having them attend just the last five minutes of the program. If they can tolerate this, increase the time to 10 minutes the next time, and then to 15 minutes, until they are able to stay in the room and participate for the entire program time.

Working with Autistic Young Children in Storytimes

Regardless of what program model you choose, there are several things to keep in mind as you work to include autistic children. Keep in mind that many of these suggestions are good practices for fostering inclusion with all children, not just those who are autistic.

- Use repetitive elements, such as the same "hello" or "goodbye" song every week.
- If a child doesn't understand how to do something, break it down into small steps for them.
- Some children will not be able to fully master the activities in your program. Aim for improved participation and praise the child's efforts and attempts, even if the child doesn't succeed.
- Show children how to do an activity in a number of ways: visually, verbally, and by modeling (demonstrating) it yourself.
- If a child has trouble with a craft or a coloring activity, ask their parent to do the activity with them, using hand-over-hand. With this method, the child holds the crayon or other item and the parent holds the child's hand and guides the crayon.

- If a child chooses not to touch Play-Doh, glue, or other substances, provide options of alternative materials that may be more tactilely pleasing to the child.
- If a child is getting upset or frustrated, it is always okay to have them leave the room with a parent or caregiver to calm down. Make sure adults are aware of where the children can go to decompress, whether it is a corner of the library or an empty meeting room.
- Set up the program room to allow space for children to get up and pace or stim, and always be accepting of these behaviors.
- Arrange the room so it is consistent and welcoming every time the program is offered. You might create a clear pathway from the door to the sitting areas, especially when in a large room, which can be overwhelming. You can designate the sitting area with carpet squares or chairs.
- Many children will benefit from sensory support options. You might have these stacked up on a table at the front of the room, or collected in a clear bucket. Headphones, sunglasses, nose plugs, weighted plush toys or lap pads, and fidgets are all good options to have for every program.

Remember that you are not expected to be an autism expert. If you don't know what to do to help a child in your storytime program, ask their parent. Be aware that sometimes the parent won't know either. Just do the best you can and keep your sense of humor. If you run into issues you don't know how to handle, turn to your partners in the autism community for assistance so you will know what to do in the future.

General Planning Considerations

There are many ways to plan a successful storytime program for young children, but you'll need to come to some decisions first. In addition to the suggestions provided in chapter 2, you may also want to consider the following questions:

How you will describe your programs?
For "Sensory-Friendly Saturdays" at the Dakota County (MN) Public Libraries, librarians decided not to include the word *storytime*. This was in direct response to feedback from families who said they felt nervous bringing their children to a storytime. While librarians know what the term means, some families might associate the word with an old-fashioned, quiet read-aloud. So the Dakota County Public Library kept all of the great elements of a sensory storytime, but rebranded it so the materials would "very plainly say what it is." As librarian Renee Grassi said, they don't want families to be deterred based on a stereotype of what a storytime is supposed to be; instead, they want people to come as they are.

What level of parent or caregiver involvement do you expect?
For young children, at least one parent or caregiver is typically required to join their children. Are there other expectations you will have for parent/caregiver participation?

How will the registration process work?
If you choose to have participants register, will you base this on the child, or on the family? Will siblings be allowed to join, and if so, do they count as a separate registrant? If you limit registration to autistic children, think about how you word this. Many young children will not yet have a diagnosis, though their parents might realize they would benefit from additional support. Instead of requiring registrants to have an autism diagnosis, for example, you could suggest that the program benefits those who have sensory sensitivities or who do better in small groups with more support.

How will you include time for community-building?
Many parents and caregivers appreciate the opportunity to connect with other families like their own. Think about ways you can build in time at the end of your program for parents and caregivers to connect with each other.

Selecting Books for Storytime

If you will be doing a program that includes autistic children, it is important to select the right books. The normal criteria you use in selecting quality books for a preschool program still apply:

- The interaction between the illustrations and the text
- The quality of both the writing and the illustrations
- An appropriate amount of text for the age or developmental stage of the children
- Illustrations that are large and clear enough to be seen by a group
- The child appeal of the title

For autistic children, we also suggest taking into account their communication styles and level of social understanding. The most successful titles for these children avoid slang, idiomatic language, and nonsense words; emphasize plot over characters and relationships; use realistic illustrations or photographs; and have uncluttered spreads with lots of white space.

Autistic children often enjoy books that are about characters they are familiar with from movies or television, even if the books don't meet some of these evaluation criteria. These include books with *Sesame Street* or Disney characters. They also love books about their special interests.

Books read aloud in storytimes should meet the criteria that we've just described. They can also be paired thematically with a sensory integration activity, something Barbara did while at the Ferguson Library. See "Appendix F: Sensory Integration Activities" for a description of the titles and activities she used.

When possible, you should purchase board books in multiples so that each child can look at a copy; or you can try adapted books (described below) to give children another layer of support.

Guidelines for Reading Books Aloud

When reading a book with text to autistic children, use Fern Sussman's "four Ss":[4]

1. *Say* less. Use simpler words that children will understand, instead of more complex words and phrases.
2. *Stress* important words by using inflection and tone of voice as you read and by defining important words as you read.
3. Go *slowly* enough so that children can follow along. Keep in mind that autistic children may take extra time to process auditory information.
4. *Show* the meaning of words. Point to pictures and make sure that the children know whom is being referenced by pronouns.

Making and Using Adapted Books

You should think about creating and using adapted picture books in your storytimes. An *adapted book* is any book that has been modified for easier use by persons with disabilities. For our purposes, an adapted picture book is one that uses pictorial icons to supplement the text, giving children a more visual way to understand the book's verbal message. Sometimes these icons are interactive, allowing children more opportunities for participation. An example of this is icons or elements of book illustrations that can be attached to or removed from

the book with Velcro. If you do incorporate interactive elements, depending on the size of your group, you can either let children follow along as you manipulate the icons, they can take turns, or you can designate a leader for each story or storytime. You may also choose to simply use static elements, permanently affixing the icons with glue or tape, or laminating them together.

If you have access to it, we recommend using icons made with Boardmaker software, as it is used widely and many children will already be familiar with the images.

FIGURE 4.1 Pete the Cat

Create an adapted "Pete the Cat" using Velcro to secure Pete's "buttons," as in this example from librarian Heather Baucum.

FIGURE 4.2 An adapted big book

The San Jose librarian Mary Nunez and library assistant Linda Keirstead use an adapted big book.

Some librarians adapt large-format picture books, which are also called *big books*. This is what the San Jose (CA) Public Library has done in its inclusive storytime program. Try to use books that have repetitive elements, which work well for autistic children.

The Paul V. Sherlock Center for Disabilities at Rhode Island College has an excellent collection of adapted materials you can download and use for educational purposes (www.ric.edu/sherlockcenter/wwslist.html). You can access some of these materials as PDF files, and some are also available as PowerPoints. You can search these materials, filtering by grade level, format, and author. If you are already using some of the titles in the Sherlock Center's collection in your storytimes, this is an easy way to get started.

Selecting Music for Storytime

The books that work most successfully for many autistic children take into account the way their brains take in and process information. This same principle applies to the selection of music. Barbara had a conversation with Dr. Dorita S. Berger, a music therapist and author of the book *Music Therapy, Sensory Integration, and the Autistic Child* (2002), about how to select music for storytime programs. Dr. Berger said that the music incorporated in programming for autistic children should have the following characteristics:

Be slow or well-paced. Well-paced music maintains a consistent tempo throughout the piece. Songs or instrumental pieces that start out slow, speed up, and then slow down again are too erratic. A tempo of 60–90 beats a minute is the best. Some music developed for children is much too fast for children with sensory-processing issues. If the brain cannot keep up with the pace of the incoming auditory information, it cannot process it, and the child won't really take in the music even if they can hear it.

Use acoustic, not electric, instruments. The purer the acoustic sound, the better the brain is able to process the auditory information. Electronically enhanced music is more than the brains of many autistic children can handle, so they will hear it as noise and tune it out.

Have simplicity of musical information. Simplicity in this case means that only a few instruments or vocalists are part of the mix. It is better to avoid music produced by large bands and orchestras, especially if singers are also involved. Children who are overwhelmed with too much auditory information can respond with boredom, tuning-out, restlessness, or anxiety. If you are playing classical music, look for music recorded by small chamber groups or duos such as a piano and violin.

Have consistent volume and don't include high-pitched sounds. You can adjust the overall volume, but be aware that some pieces have sudden loud elements that can produce a flight-or-fight response. The sudden sound of high-pitched notes in particular can be jarring. Alternatively, if the work has sections that are too soft, the child may just tune out.

Use child singers. Children like to hear voices that sound like theirs.

Background Music in Storytime

You may wish to incorporate background music, not sing-along songs, into your storytime programs. For storytimes with autistic children in the group, Dr. Berger recommends:

- Bach and Handel's music (but not their orchestral pieces)
- Mozart and Hayden string quartets
- Mozart piano sonatas
- Schubert piano sonatas
- Brahms piano and violin sonatas
- Anything by Ravel or Debussy
- Songs by the Beatles (but avoid boisterous rock songs in general)
- American Indian flute music
- A cappella vocal groups
- Spanish, Latin American, and South American instrumental music

Sing-along Music and Other Songs for Storytime

You may want to use music in your storytime programs that children can sing along with, or that takes a more central role in the program. Music that has patterns or repetitive elements will work well to hold attention, both from autistic children and any other children in the room. Two examples of classic stories that have repetitive song structures are "Old MacDonald Had a Farm" and "There Was an Old Lady Who Swallowed a Fly." Librarian Heather Baucum uses both of these songs in her storytimes because their musical patterns are familiar and enjoyable for autistic children. As an added bonus, she lets children lead the verse of "Old MacDonald" when she references a favorite interest. For example, one child loves transportation, so Heather always includes the verse "Old MacDonald had a truck," and asks him to lead the group as they sing.

Many books have songs incorporated within them, and these can be very popular with children. One example is the *Pete the Cat* series by authors Eric

Litwin, a former special education teacher, and James Dean. These books use variations of the same catchy, repetitive song. *Pete the Cat* books were designed to be multisensory, and to keep children engaged through music and movement.

Created by two children's librarians, Jbrary (www.jbrary.com) is an excellent resource for song ideas and simple corresponding movements. Their YouTube channel features a wide assortment of simple songs, many with repetitive elements, with both librarians demonstrating fingerplays and movements. You can search by theme to find songs that work with your programming.

You can also check out some of the following well-known children's musicians for songs that might work well with autistic children in your storytimes. Many of these songs have been used successfully in the Ferguson Library, and all are available to purchase as CDs or to stream online:

- Many of the *Laurie Berkner Band*'s songs work well for sensory storytimes. Try "Balance Beam," "Clean It Up," "I've Been Working on the Railroad," and "The Story of My Feelings." You can order their CDs online or stream through their YouTube channel.
- *Raffi*'s music has been loved by children and parents for a generation. Songs we especially like are "Brush Your Teeth," "Baa, Baa Black Sheep," "Mr. Sun," "The Sharing Song," and "Five Little Frogs." "The More We Get Together" is a wonderful song to use at the beginning of a program. "De Colores" is a lovely song in Spanish that will be familiar to your Latinx families. "Thanks a Lot" is a good song to play during a quiet meditative time at the end of a program. Raffi also has a nice, quiet version of "Twinkle, Twinkle." Pick the songs from the original albums rather than the concert versions since the concert albums tend to have orchestral backup. Again, you can purchase the songs as CDs or stream them through a service such as Spotify.
- *Hap Palmer* is a musician with a degree in dance education, and is a master at combining music and movement in gentle songs that help young children learn. The songs "Touch," "The Circle," and "Turn Around" and their accompanying activities would make good additions to a storytime. Palmer also has a streaming music video collection on YouTube.
- *Jim Gill* has many albums full of "movement" songs that encourage children to dance and move their bodies. Try incorporating some of the songs from his "Most Celebrated Songs" CD collections.

As you might have realized, many songs that you probably already use in your general storytimes work well for all children, including those who are autistic. You probably already have a strong digital or CD collection that you can draw from as you plan your storytime programs. Even so, be sure to preview any song before you play it in a storytime program that includes autistic children. Additionally, if you create a streaming playlist of songs through a service such as Pandora or Spotify, be sure to pay for a subscription, so the music is not

A Great Idea: Story Cubes

Story cubes are a set of dice, and each die has a picture on each of its sides. Each roll of the dice yields a different set of pictures, and these can be used as a starting point for a story or conversation. Commercial sets of story cubes are readily available, or you can make your own. In one variation, you can use story cubes paired with the "Old MacDonald" song. You can make story cubes out of small tissue boxes covered in brown paper, like the ones used by the Alvin Sherman Library. For "Old MacDonald," paste a different animal picture on each surface of the cube, as shown in the figure below. Each child in turn tosses the cube, and the animal facing up is the one featured in the next song verse. Coloring pages' line drawings (available free online) can be substituted for Boardmaker pictures on the cubes if that software is not available.

"Old MacDonald" story cubes
from the Alvin Sherman Library

interrupted by jarring advertisements. You don't have to be sophisticated musically to tell if there are loud surprise elements, if too much verbal information is presented too quickly, if the piece is boring, or if you can't make out the lyrics. If you can notice these things, you can be pretty sure that a child with sensory issues will not be able to respond to the music in the way it was intended.

Selecting Other Materials for Storytime

Along with selecting books to read and music to engage with, you also need to provide other activities and materials that will support your autistic storytime attendees. These materials include visual schedules, beanbags, fidgets, and adaptive craft equipment.

Visual Schedules

Visual schedules allow children to follow along with the program, and to prepare in advance for transitions. Using Boardmaker software if you have it, you can produce individual 8½" × 11" pictures for each activity and a separate 8½" × 11" schedule that includes all of the activities. Laminate all of the visuals or place them in plastic sheet protectors. Attach the corresponding visual to a flannel board with Velcro as an activity begins, and remove it when the activity is completed.

Incorporating Beanbags

Beanbags are a fun and useful addition to all storytimes, and they offer benefits for autistic children. They can be used in tossing games to help children work on their hand/eye coordination, color recognition, and other skills. They can be placed on shoulders or heads while children march to music, helping the kids work on balance and get some proprioceptive input. Reasonably priced, pre-made beanbags are readily available through school specialty stores and other online retailers or, if you like to DIY, it is easy to make your own beanbags with fabric squares and rice or small beans as filler. Try fabrics with a variety of textures, like washable velvet and corduroy, for some sensory input. Choose a variety of colors or patterns, and make sure the beanbags are small enough to be held comfortably by your storytime attendees. You can even take old socks, fill them partway, and tie the ends shut. Try marching to any lively music with beanbags, or use classic songs like "The Ants Go Marching." You can also try a beanbag activity like this one from Storytime Stuff:

At the Circus

Place a masking tape line on the floor to act as a tightrope. Invite the children to balance their beanbags on their heads as they walk along the line. If they drop them, encourage them to pick them up and keep trying.

> *With my beanbag on my head,*
> *I stand so very tall.*
> *I walk along my own tightrope*
> *And will not let it fall.*[5]

You can also easily find action songs for children online that feature beanbags. If you use recorded songs, make sure they meet the criteria for music outlined above. Try "The Bean Bag" from *Can a Jumbo Jet Sing the Alphabet?* by Hap Palmer, "Bean Bag Parade" from *Action Songs*, Vol. 2 by Tumble Tots, or some of the songs like "Body Cross, Applesauce" or "I Have a Beanbag" on music therapist Rachel's Rambach's website, "Listen Learn Music" (www.listenlearnmusic .com).

In addition to beanbags, you should consider play tunnels, items to walk and balance on, a parachute, egg shakers, scarves, bubbles, and similar items. You can find or create many storytime and sensory integration activities that use these items, and you are likely to have many of them already. You should also keep a supply of plain, inexpensive, white paper plates on hand. These can be used as stepping stones or instruments, and kids can draw on them instead of on paper. They can also be the basis for numerous craft projects.

Incorporating Fidgets

You should have fidget toys on hand and let children pick one they like as they need it during the program. Or you can place simple fidget items like squeeze balls at tables and workstations. If you have chair seating at a program, consider tying a stretchy band around the chair's legs for a child to kick during the program. This can help the child burn off some energy, as well as focus during the program.

Adapting Crafts

A book-related program for younger elementary students will often include a craft activity as well as the reading of a book. If you want your crafts to work for autistic children, it is important to take their possible tactile sensitivities, communication styles, and fine motor skills into account. The following are some tips for craft activities with autistic children:

- Provide a visual schedule of the project—something that looks like the pictures in a cookbook—so children can see what each step looks like. This is also a good way to reinforce the concept of sequencing. Alternatively, you can provide a checklist of the steps in the project.
- Provide alternatives to glue (like double-sided tape) and gooey paint (like watercolor pencils) for children who have tactile sensitivity.
- Try to avoid objects like sequins that are too small for a child with fine motor issues to manipulate. Instead, provide other materials that require less precision, like large stickers.
- Invest in a couple of pairs of adaptive scissors, which can be very helpful for children with fine motor difficulties. Adaptive scissors may require less hand strength to open and close. Some operate by pressing down on them.
- Have large-size or easy-grip crayons and markers available. Paper with lines or grids to guide writing will also be helpful, as will pencil grips.
- Have another staff member, volunteer, or parent circle the room to help children with their crafts. All children want help if they are frustrated with a task, and if that help is not available, frustration can lead to a meltdown.
- Sharing can be a tough concept to learn for all children. You can help reduce frustrations by dividing the craft materials into baskets or placing them on paper plates before the program. Give each child their own set of materials, and label the baskets with the materials they contain.
- Have a clearly designated place for washing hands. If your meeting room does not have a sink, try an alternative like wet wipes.

Storytime Kits to-Go

You can help support families to continue the great work you've started by offering them storytime kits to-go. The Pasadena (CA) Public Library has Sensory Storytime Kits that families can check out to enjoy a prepackaged program at home. Each kit contains up to three books, a sensory toy, and an activity or music CD, all focused on a common theme.[6] Jen Taggart has also developed kits to-go. Her kits correspond to some of her virtual storytimes, allowing children to engage with the multisensory aspects of the story while participating from home.

Virtual Storytimes

Librarian Jen Taggart notes that making story-times accessible to your patrons *virtually* is a very important consideration, so even if you choose to host online storytimes live, try to record and post them so children and families can access them later on demand. In a survey that Taggart's library implemented, most patrons reported preferring on-demand program options. These have other benefits as well; prerecording storytimes avoids some internet connection issues that can be encountered during streaming, and also allows families and children to access the sessions during the time that fits best with their schedules.

Though children don't get the full benefit of socialization with this format, virtual storytimes are still a valuable service to provide for families who are unable to get to the library but still want to work on developing early literacy skills. Additionally, some autistic children may find it easier to engage in an online storytime, perhaps building their comfort level and ability to attend later face-to-face library programs, if they are available. As Taggart says, "some kids will stim more when they're outside of the house, but when they're at home in a comfortable, familiar environment, that may lead to their being able to engage better with the program." For such children and their families or caregivers, these online storytimes are an excellent option.

You can provide a list of objects that families and caregivers can have available for children before they access the online storytime, allowing you to incorporate sensory activities into the program. Make sure these objects are ones that are commonly found in homes; for example, a small potted plant to correspond with a gardening story. Alternatively, you can do what Miss Rachel does during virtual storytimes at William Jeanes Memorial Library (Lafayette, PA). During the videos, she gives viewers instructions for alternatives to the scarves and shakers used in the library during her in-person program. Viewers can pause the video, get the object, and return to the storytime when they are ready (https://jeaneslibrary.org/children/childrens-storytimes). Another option is to provide storytime kits to-go that align with your storytime themes. These are described in more detail in the next text box.

For more information about general virtual storytime practices, ALA's Association for Library Services to Children has a helpful "Virtual Storytime Services Guide" (www.ala.org/alsc/virtual-storytime-services-resource-guide). You can also refer to the *Adaptive Umbrella* blog for adaptive literacy resources (https://adaptiveumbrella.blogspot.com/).

Four Sample Sensory Storytime Programs

Some public libraries start a storytime just for autistic children, and then learn that their communities are better served by building inclusive elements into all storytimes. This was the case for both the Alvin Sherman Joint Use Library at Nova Southeastern University and the Henrico County Public Library in Richmond, Virginia. The Alvin Sherman Library now keeps a consistent weekly storytime schedule so autistic children can participate whenever it works best for their families, and the library no longer offers a targeted autism storytime, since all storytimes are now accessible to all. Henrico County librarians felt that their sensory storytime, open only to children with an autism diagnosis, was successful but that it excluded other children who might also benefit. Now, their sensory storytime is marketed for children of all abilities. Though autism is not specifically mentioned in the program description, Henrico County librarians ensure that autistic patrons will be supported. Their librarians want children to be able to predict what is going to happen when they walk in the room, so the components are exactly the same in each of the six weekly sessions. Most of the content stays the same from session to session as well, with perhaps the introduction of a new song and flannel board activity. They always incorporate both a small and large motor skills activity, and there is always a movement experience or activity book.

Basic Elements of a Sensory Storytime Program

Sensory storytimes should all include the same basic elements:

1. Welcome song or greeting that is used consistently for each session
2. Introduction activity
3. Sensory activities
4. Stories read aloud
5. Songs or fingerplays
6. Closing song or activity that is used consistently for each session

This is just a basic template that can be modified for your use; the order of nearly every element can be swapped (with the exception of the welcome, introductions, and closing activities). Some libraries incorporate crafts or time for sensory "free play." Just make sure to keep your programs consistent so attendees know what to expect each time they attend.

The rest of this chapter provides detailed descriptions and program elements of four different sensory storytimes tailored for autistic children. They were developed for the Ferguson Library (Stamford, CT), the Henrico County Public Library (Richmond, VA), the Deerfield Public Library (Deerfield, IL), and the Bloomfield Township Public Library (Bloomfield Township, MI). You should dig into these program models and think about which approaches will work the best in your library. You might find that you prefer to mix and match elements that you like from these program examples, or enhance these models with more of the best practices you've read about. And, as described in the previous chapter, for every program you should:

- Provide sensory supports and a visual schedule.
- Control the environment and minimize distractions.
- Build in predictability with program elements that repeat each session.

SENSORY STORYTIME

Ferguson Library, Stamford, Connecticut
Designed by librarian Barbara Klipper (some activities designed by
special education teacher and program leader Gabriela Marcus)

Frequency: This program was offered as a series of three or four meetings, with four series offered in a year. It has also been offered on a once-a-month basis. All meetings are on Saturday mornings for one hour.

Ages: 3–5

Registration: Required, and limited to 10 to 12 children

This inclusive program was originally funded by a grant from a local organization called Abilis. Parents were asked to actively participate with their children and to attend without siblings if at all possible.

What You'll Need

- Educubes, small round vinyl mats (from matsmatsmats.com), and stools
- Balance beam (tactile path from www.funandfunction.com; Starter Beams from www.especialneeds.com or tape)
- Half-pound weighted beanbags (from www.funandfunction.com, or homemade)
- Toothettes (available from Amazon.com) or inexpensive toothbrushes
- TheraBands or extra-large rubber bands
- Visual schedule (made with Boardmaker software)
- A laminator or plastic sheet protectors
- Name tags made from boy and girl puppet Ellison die cuts
- Velcro dots
- Multiple copies of board books (when the title is available in this format)
- Various supplies for the book-related sensory activities (rice bins, ice cube trays, etc.)
- Rubber stamps, ink pads, and paper (or stickers)
- CD player and CDs
- Large flannel board
- T-shirt shapes cut from felt, or a large sensory ball
- Sample Program Plan

As parents and children arrive, ask parents to check their names on an attendance sheet and take the children's name tags, which are made of die-cut shapes with a Velcro dot on the back. Parents help their children place the name tags on the flannel board. Toys are available for play while early arrivals wait for the program to begin; the toys are placed out of sight when the program starts.

SAMPLE PROGRAM PLAN

WELCOME

Ask the children to sit in a semicircle on the Educubes. Pad the cubes with cushions if needed. Ask parents to sit behind their children on stools. Give each child-adult pair a copy of the activity schedule to review.

Hello Song
"Hello Everyone"

> *Hello everyone, how are you, how are you, how are you?*
> *Hello everyone, how are you, how are you today?*

Referring to the name tags, sing the song again to each child in turn, using their name.

Welcome Activity: Shirt Song

Cut T-shirt shapes out of felt in a variety of colors. Arrange them on a table. In turn, ask each child to name the color of the shirt they are wearing. When they name the color (or get help identifying the color), ask them to pick up the felt shirt in that color and put it on the flannel board. As they do this, everyone sings:

"Shirt Song" (to the tune of "Mary Wore Her Red Dress")

> *[Child's name] has a [color] shirt, [color] shirt, [color] shirt,*
> *[Child's name] is wearing a [color] shirt,*
> *And they are here today.*

Roll the Ball (Alternate Welcome Activity)

Roll a large sensory ball to each child in turn, asking him to roll, kick, or throw the ball back:

"Roll the Ball" (to the tune of "Row, Row, Row Your Boat")

> *Roll, roll, roll the ball, roll the ball to [child's name].*
> *[Child's name four times], roll it back to me.*

SENSORY ACTIVITY CHOICES

Include three to four of these in each program. If you are doing a series with the same children, repeat the same activities in the same order each meeting. Some sensory integration activity choices are described below. For other ideas, refer to the books and websites listed in "Appendix F: Sensory Integration Activities."

Stretch Song (with TheraBands)

Give a five- to six-foot-long piece of TheraBand to each child. Show the children how to anchor the band under the Educube or the child's feet with equal lengths on both sides. Ask the children to hold an end of the band in each hand and pull. Model what you want the children to do. Encourage everyone to sing together. Two children (or a parent and child) can hold opposite ends of the TheraBand and pull back and forth to the music for "Row, Row, Row Your Boat." Songs that work well with TheraBands are: "Head, Shoulders, Knees, and Toes," "Itsy Bitsy Spider," "Row, Row, Row Your Boat," and "The Noble Duke of York." The idea is to do the work of pulling and releasing the band rather than to do the traditional movements that go with these songs. You can also do this activity with extra-large rubber bands.

Brush Your Teeth (Oral Motor Activity)

Give each child an individually wrapped toothette swab or toothbrush. Play the song "Brush Your Teeth" from *Raffi's Singable Songs for the Very Young* CD and model brushing teeth with the toothette. Parents whose kids have food texture aversions or other related sensory issues could also rub their lips and cheeks with the swabs to provide oral stimulation. Describe this to the parents as the toothettes are distributed. Ask parents to make sure that their children don't eat the sponges on the toothettes. Alternative oral motor activities include blowing bubbles, or whistles, or blowing cotton balls using drinking straws.

Beanbag March

Give each child two half-pound weighted beanbags. Play "Bean Bag Parade" by Tumble Tots from the *Action Songs, Volume 2* CD. Model placing a bag on each shoulder and holding it in place, then lead everyone in marching around the room. If a child can't do this on their own, ask parents to assist by holding the bags so the child feels what it is like to move with the weights. Many autistic children use weighted vests or other items to provide proprioceptive input.

Balance Beam

Encourage the children to do this activity in bare feet, especially if you use a tactile path or other beam with texture, but if they are uncomfortable, allow them to keep their shoes and socks on. Invite the children to walk on the beam to Laurie Berkner's "Balance Beam" song from the *Rocketship Run* CD. Direct the children to walk slowly, keep space between them, feel the texture of the path, walk sideways, and so on. Children can walk on the beam alone, hold a parent's hand, or be given as much physical support as they need.

Book

Distribute board book copies, if available, of the title you will read that day. Ask children who can to read along. Invite parents to assist the children with holding the books, turning the pages, and noticing the illustrations. If the title is not available as a board book, then only the librarian has a copy, and the librarian does all of the reading. The visual schedule shows all of the books that will be read during a program series, so that children know in advance which book will be read each week. Parents can take those books home to read with their children before the program.

Book-Related Sensory Activity

Collect the books and lead the children to the area that is set up for the sensory activity that thematically matches the book you just read. Additional songs and activities that fit the theme can be added to extend the program. The books and activities used in the Ferguson Library program are detailed in Appendix F.

CLEANUP

After each activity, invite parents and children to collect the materials and put them away. After the book-related activity, the adults also help with dismantling the balance beam and putting the Educubes away. The adults sing:

> *Clean up, clean up, everybody, everywhere.*
> *Clean up, clean up, everybody do your share.*

Laurie Berkner's "Clean It Up" song from the *Buzz Buzz* CD can be played during the cleanup session at the end of the program.

FREE PLAY TIME

Bring out a variety of puzzles, sensory toys, and fidgets for the children to play with on their own for about ten minutes. The parents can use this time to network with each other or to ask the leader questions.

GOODBYE

Offer one or two of the emotion-faced hand stamps from a Melissa & Doug Expressions Stamper set to each child in turn, letting each child choose the stamp they want to use. Have paper available for the stamps for children who don't want to have the stamp on their skin. You can use stickers instead of stamps, if you prefer.

SENSORY STORYTIME

Henrico County Public Library, Richmond, Virginia
Designed by librarian Erin Lovelace

Frequency: Once weekly for six sessions; two-week break between sessions

Ages: 1–5

Registration: None needed

What You'll Need

- Visual schedule: Make a picture for each song/book/activity, using Boardmaker, and Velcro them to a display. Each picture is removed as the activity ends. The schedule is shown frequently throughout the program.
- Mats/carpet squares to mark out personal space
- TheraBands
- A set of board books, one for each participant you expect (their kits have 25)
- Feathers
- Bubble machine
- No-spill bubble containers
- Toys

SAMPLE PROGRAM PLAN

WELCOME AND REVIEW OF VISUAL SCHEDULE

Hello Song to the Tune of "London Bridge"

> *Hi, hello, how are you?*
> *How are you? How are you?*
> *Hi, hello, how are you?*
> *How are you today?*

(practice/encourage waving and saying hello to each other)

Fingerplay/Song

"Where Is Thumbkin"
Sing and act out fingerplay with children and their caregivers following along.

Whole Body Play

"Row, Row, Row Your Boat"
Encourage the caregivers and their children to face each other, hold hands, and pull each other back and forth in a rowing motion with small or large movement, depending on the child's abilities and preference.

Stretch Song (with TheraBands): "Twinkle Twinkle Little Star"
Hand out TheraBands to be pulled and stretched during this song, anchored by the child's feet or a chair.

Book

The Itsy Bitsy Spider by Rosemary Wells
This is shared as a board book set. Each child receives their own book, and caregivers are encouraged to read along with the librarian.

Fingerplay

After reading the book, continue the activity by singing "The Itsy Bitsy Spider" and incorporating fingerplay.

Counting and Jumping

"Ladybug Spots"

> *The Ladybug has spots*
> *The ladybug has spots*
> *Can you count the number of*
> *This ladybug's spots?*

Hold up a ladybug picture or toy at the end of each round, and count the dots. Then encourage the children to jump while you count to that number a second time. Repeat this for three rounds of ladybugs.

Song

"Head, Shoulders, Knees, and Toes"
Incorporate a local "crowd favorite" song; this one is a favorite for Henrico County kids.

Whole Body Play

"The Elevator Song" from Jbrary
Find out what interests your kids have and build in something just for them. Henrico County has a regular attendee who loves elevators, so they keep him engaged with this song near the end of the storytime. The "Old MacDonald" song, with a child's special interest substituting for an animal, such as the truck example we described earlier, is also a good option.

SENSORY ACTIVITY: ORAL PRACTICE, BLOWING BUBBLES

Give every child who wants one a no-spill toddler container of bubbles to practice with. Some children who have oral-motor challenges might find blowing bubbles tough. You can also use a bubble machine during this activity as an alternative.

CLOSING SONG

"Skinamarink"

FREE PLAY TIME

After the storytime, bring in a variety of toys for kids to play with while the parents talk. Use a combination of traditional toys, like trucks and balls, as well as some other items like water to paint with, laundry baskets to climb in and out of, materials to build with, and objects that spin.

Based on your community's needs, you might find that offering some programming specifically for groups of autistic children is the best approach. These next two program models are good examples.

SENSORY STORYTIME AND SENSORY PLAY

Deerfield Public Library, Deerfield, Illinois
Designed by librarian Julia Frederick

Frequency: Monthly; Fridays from 11:30 a.m. to 12:30 p.m.

Ages: No requirement

Registration: None needed

In Deerfield, Illinois, librarian Julia Frederick offers a monthly storytime program just for autistic children. She finds that many of the children who attend this storytime also attend the general Saturday morning storytime, perhaps because their experiences in the autism storytime have helped them to develop a level of comfort with the library and the storytime format generally.

This drop-in program, run by one librarian, is regularly attended by 7–10 children and their parents or caregivers. Each session consists of 30 minutes of storytime and 30 minutes of sensory play. Since this is a drop-in program, you should ask caregivers and children for their names as they come in and make name tags for them. Add an element of participation by letting kids choose stickers to put on their name tags. To set up the program, place 5–10 BackJack chairs in a semicircle facing the large flannel board, and place the visual schedule on the flannel board. Set up the Sensory Play stations at the back of the room.

What You'll Need for the Sensory Storytime

- Visual schedule
- Large flannel board
- Felt flannel pieces
- BackJack chairs
- Name tags
- A variety of fidgets and noise-canceling headphones
- Portable speaker or CD player
- Shaker eggs
- Rhythm sticks

What You'll Need for Sensory Play

- Play-Doh (offer alternatives for kids who don't like the feel of Play-Doh)
- Dough tools
- Water Beads (these plastic marbles expand when wet; search online or buy them from Lakeshore)
- Plastic animals
- Shaving cream
- Water bowl
- Butcher paper
- Coloring sheets
- Easy-hold egg-shaped crayons
- LEGO Duplo Blocks
- Sensory blocks (try see-through blocks, or those that stick together)
- Sight and Sound Tubes (clear tubes filled with objects of different weights, shapes, and sizes; available from Lakeshore, or build your own)

SAMPLE PROGRAM PLAN

At the beginning of the program, go through the visual schedule of activities on the large flannel board. Explain to everyone that as you complete each activity, you will remove it from the large schedule to signal the end of that activity.

WELCOME

Begin by teaching the American Sign Language (ASL) signs for "hello," "friends," and "time." You can find the signs for these at https://www.youtube.com/watch?v=tKCGF2hvq3I. Sing the following song twice to give kids a chance to practice.

"Hello Friends" (with ASL signing; example available on Jbrary)

> *Hello friends, hello friends, hello friends,*
> *It's time to say hello.*

Book and Flannel Board Activity

Cat's Colors by Jane Cabrera

Give each child one or two flannel squares in different colors and have them bring their squares to the large flannel board when the color is introduced in the book. Encourage children to perform this task with statements like, "You can do it! Great job!" Offer hints or prompts if needed to assist children in identifying the color of their squares. Once the book has been read and the activity completed, count how many colors made it on to the board.

Songs

Sing **"Shake Your Shakers"** with shaker eggs to the tune of "London Bridge":

> *Shake your shakers, shake shake shake,*
> *Shake shake shake, shake shake shake.*

Shake your shakers, shake shake shake,
Shake your shakers.

Repeat "Shake Your Shakers" with hands held high, then low, shaking fast, and then slow.

Sing **"If You're Happy and You Know It"** with the shaker eggs:

If you're happy and you know it, give a shake!
If you're happy and you know it, give a shake!
If you're happy and you know it, then your face will surely show it!
If you're happy and you know it, give a shake!

Play **"Alouette"** from *Outrageous Orange from The Learning Groove* by Mr. Eric & Mr. Michael.

Walk around the room with a basket and have children return their shakers to complete the activity.

Book
Grandma's Tiny House: A Counting Story! by JaNay Brown-Wood

Fingerplays
- "Open Shut Them"
- "The Itsy Bitsy Spider"

FIGURE 4.3 Sensory Storytime
Librarian Julia Frederick leads Sensory Storytime using a visual schedule

Book

From Head to Toe by Eric Carle

Have children and caregivers try the movements in this book. Offer up suggestions for alternative movements if a movement in the book is too difficult. (Example: Instead of kicking their legs like a donkey, suggest stomping feet or clapping hands—whatever is comfortable for them.)

Flannel Board

"Where's the Mouse?"

The flannel pieces for this activity consist of seven common shapes and one mouse shape. The shapes are a square, a rectangle, a heart, a star, a circle, a triangle, and a diamond—all in different colors. First, introduce the mouse and have everyone say hello. Then, go through the shapes and their colors. Ask the children if they know what shape/color the flannel piece is before telling them. Give hints if needed; for example, for yellow, try saying something like "This is the color of a banana. Do you know what it is called?" Finally, hide the mouse behind one of the shapes while everyone closes their eyes or looks away from the flannel board. Have children guess where the mouse is hiding and see who can guess correctly the shape and color the mouse is hiding behind. After each guess, count to three before the big reveal.

Bubbles

Play light, happy music while blowing bubbles at children. Give children the option of having bubbles blown near them or not.

GOODBYE

Sing **"We Wave Goodbye Like This"** to the tune "Farmer in the Dell."

> *We wave goodbye like this,*
> *We wave goodbye like this,*
> *We clap our hands for all our friends,*
> *We wave goodbye like this*

FREE PLAY TIME

After the goodbye song, explain the stations that have been set up for Sensory Play. Allow children and caregivers to pick the stations they wish to explore. See below for more information about Sensory Play.

Station 1: Play-Doh and Dough Tools

Let children and caregivers make and play with Play-Doh and dough tools. Provide an alternative modeling substance as well that is more appealing to those who are tactilely defensive.

Station 2: Water Beads, Plastic Animals, Shaving Cream, Water Bowl with Water

Remind caregivers that this is a messy station! Lay down a plastic tablecloth on a table and put out pre-soaked Water Beads, small plastic animals, shaving cream, and a water bowl filled with water. Spray the shaving cream on the table and let children cover the animals in shaving cream and water beads and then "wash and clean" the animals with water.

Station 3: Butcher Paper, Coloring Sheets, Easy-Hold Egg-Shaped Crayons

Cover a table with butcher paper and let children color the paper and coloring sheets with crayons.

Station 4: LEGO Duplo Blocks, Sensory Blocks, Sight and Sound Tubes

Place the Duplo Blocks, sensory blocks, and Sight and Sound Tubes on the floor for free play.

SENSEATIONAL STORYTIME: "LET'S GO" THEME

Bloomfield Township Public Library, Bloomfield Township, Michigan
Designed by youth librarian Jen Taggart

Frequency: Monthly during the school year

Description and Ages: A monthly storytime developed for children with intellectual and/or developmental disabilities. Visuals, interactive preschool-level stories, adaptive movement, and multisensory activities engage the senses. For children ages 3–10, with a favorite adult.

Registration: Yes, limited to 12 children and their caregivers

What You'll Need
- Visual schedule
- A textured, sensory ball
- Flannel board with flannel train car, bus, dog, and cat manipulatives
- Steering wheels made from paper plate cutouts
- Long piece of construction paper roll for the "bridge"
- Stretch bands (latex-free)
- Circle-time parachute
- Toy cars or trucks, and gluten-free Play-Doh for play activity after the program

SAMPLE PROGRAM PLAN

WELCOME

Say "hello" and explain the visual schedule.

Introduce children and caregivers to the visual schedule so they know what to expect during your time together.

Song

"The Storytime Ball" sung to the tune of "Wheels on the Bus"
(Roll the ball back and forth to each child):

> *The story time ball rolls back and forth,*
> *back and forth, back and forth.*
> *The story time ball rolls back and forth,*
> *Let's see who it found. Hi ____!*
> *Now roll it back to me.*

(Keep rolling the ball back and forth until each child has said their name.)

Mindfulness Activity

"Hot Air Balloon" Breath
Give the following instructions and ask the children to follow along:

> *Stand tall or sit up.*
> *Place your hands on your stomach.*
> *Breathe in and feel your stomach rise (blow the balloon up, up, up).*
> *Breathe out and feel your stomach (the balloon) go in.*

Repeat, and then relax and release the balloon.

Flannel Board

"Clickety-Clack" (adding flannel train car pieces on to a flannel board)
(See detailed instructions for the pieces by searching "clickety-clack" on the *Mel's Desk* blog: www.melissa.depperfamily.net/blog/.)

> *Clickety-clack, clickety clack,*
> *Here comes the train on the railroad track!*
>
> *Clickety-clunn, clickety-clunn,*
> *Here comes Engine number one.*
> *Clickety-clew, clickety-clew,*
> *Here comes Coal Car number two.*
> *Clickety-clee, clickety-clee,*
> *Here comes Box Car number three.*
> *Clickety-clore, clickety-clore,*
> *Here comes Tank Car number four.*
> *Clickety-clive, clickety-clive,*

Here comes Coach Car number five.
Clickety-clicks, clickedty-clicks,
Here's the Caboose, that's number six.
Clickety-clack, clickety-clack,
There goes the train on the railroad track!
Choo-chooooooo!

Book

The Bridge Is Up! by Babs Bell
Give each child a paper-plate steering wheel so they can "drive" across the "bridge." Have grownups hold up the paper "bridge" and place it on the floor when the kids can cross.

Stretch Song (with TheraBands)

"Row, Row, Row Your Boat"

> *Row, row, row your boat*
> *gently down the stream,*
> *Merrily, merrily, merrily, merrily,*
> *life is but a dream.*

(Repeat, pulling back and forth on the stretch band "oars" to row our boat.)

Book

My Bus by Byron Barton
Use the flannel bus and animal manipulatives. Give each child a flannel dog or cat to add to the bus.

Whole Body Play

Parachute Activity: "Wheels on the Bus"
Kids can sit under the parachute or hold the parachute.

> *The wheels on the bus go round and round,*
> *round and round, round and round.*
> *The wheels on the bus go round and round,*
> *all over town.*
> *(parachute goes around)*
>
> *The doors on the bus go open and shut . . .*
> *(parachute goes in and out)*
> *The windows on the bus go up and down . . .*
> *(parachute goes up and down)*
> *The people on the bus go bumpity bump . . .*
> *(Shake that parachute!)*

GOODBYE

Stretch: "Tickle the Clouds"

> *Tickle the clouds.*
> *Tickle your toes.*
> *Turn around and tickle your nose (or turn head side to side, if seated)*
> *Reach down low.*
> *Reach up high.*
> *Story time's over.*
> *Wave goodbye!*

FREE PLAY TIME

Each SENSEational Storytime ends with roughly 10–15 minutes of free play or sensory discovery. For free play, provide a variety of toys (some adaptive) and/or therapeutic materials related to the storytime's theme, for example, toy cars and trucks. Sensory discovery might include sensory bins or sensory materials (such as gluten-free Play-Doh) for interactive and/or independent exploration and discovery.

This concludes our survey of four recommended storytime programs. For some additional programs you can replicate, search "book and play" on Jen Taggart's blog, *Adaptive Umbrella*, or search "sensory storytime" on the Pasadena Public Library's blog (www.pasadena-library.net/kids) to see examples from librarian Marie Plug.

Final Thoughts

Some of the programs we featured in this section received their initial funding from grants through the LSTA, Friends of the Library groups, or foundations. These grants can be helpful in paying for start-up costs; for example, the initial purchases of software like Boardmaker, supplies, and seating options. We provide a list of possible sources of grants in "Appendix D: Potential Funding Sources for Programs" if you want to seek this type of funding for your program. However, if you aren't able to dedicate time and resources to grant-writing, there are many ways you can modify a program to fit within the resources you have. Also, keep in mind that part of a culture of inclusion is a commitment from the administration to put resources into services and programs for all community members. You should advocate for the inclusion of these programs in your library's regular budget. If the library's staff has been trained and brought on board, it should be possible to get a line item to fund this work. But however you acquire funding, remember that the models provided in this chapter are what work in the communities that do them, and you can customize these ideas or find others that will work best for you, given the resources your library has and the needs of the community you serve.

NOTES

1. Kathleen Campana et al., "Early Literacy in Library Storytimes: A Study of Measures of Effectiveness," *Library Quarterly* 86, no. 4 (2016).

2. Sean F. Reardon and Ximena A. Portilla, "Recent Trends in Income, Racial, and Ethnic School Readiness Gaps at Kindergarten Entry," *AERA Open* 2, no. 3 (2016), doi: 2332858416657343.

3. Every Child Ready to Read, http://everychildreadytoread.org.

4. Fern Sussman, "A Very Short List of Recommended Books," in *Talkability: People Skills for Verbal Children on the Autism Spectrum—A Guide for Parents* (Toronto: Hanen Centre, 2006), 107.

5. Storytime Stuff, "Brilliant Bean Bags," https://storytimestuff.wordpress.com/2013/07/14/brilliant-bean-bags.

6. Marie Plug, "Sensory Storytime," *Kids Blog*, Pasadena Public Library, January 27, 2017, http://pasadena-library.net/kids/2017/sensory-storytime.

Programming for School-Age Children

MANY YOUTH SERVICES LIBRARIANS NOW KNOW THAT STORYTIMES are important for young autistic children, and they focus their efforts on this type of program. But what happens when these children grow older, given the fact that they would still benefit from library programming? In this chapter, we provide program ideas and services for what we're referring to as "school-age children," or those who are about 5 to 13 years old. The types of programs we consider include book discussions and activities such as yoga, gardening, and gaming, and we introduce a number of these options. Finally, we'll discuss how to make your summer reading programs more inclusive.

Best Practices for Book Discussions

You should think about ways of incorporating the best practices we introduced in chapter 3 to help make any book discussion program more inclusive for autistic children. For example, you can use visuals, give the children notice about transitions, and keep the group size small. You should have advance registration, and send out any materials to children in advance so they can prepare. You can provide options for craft activities; see the information about adapted crafts in chapter 4. You can build in a sensory break, allowing participants to walk in the back of the room, push against the wall, jump in place, or engage in their preferred self-stimulating behavior (or stim). Stimming is an important tool that many autistic people use to self-regulate, and attempts to reduce or eliminate stims could actually be harmful. Try to create a culture in the program in which children know these behaviors are acceptable, even during the program, if they need stimulation or centering.

When you design the program, do your best to ensure that all of its elements are age-appropriate. For example, you might consider providing one or more of these seating options that help older kids:

- Ball chairs in your program room can be very cool, and all kids and teens will love them, especially for gaming. These chairs are made up of a large inflatable ball, like the kind you'd see at a gym, placed in some kind of frame.
- Tactile air cushions placed on chairs provide good sensory input. You can find them online from a number of suppliers.
- Wobble stools are a lot of fun for all wiggly kids, allowing plenty of movement while being safely tethered to the ground.

Book Discussions for Younger School-Age Children (Grades K–2)

Book discussions can easily be designed to be inclusive or more supportive for autistic children. Book discussions for the K–2 set are really just a variation on storytimes. The choice of books will be different than for younger kids, and elements like fingerplays and nursery rhymes might be replaced by poems, music-making, movement, and other enhancements that make a storytime program age-appropriate for these children. Whether you are working with an inclusive group or a targeted group of autistic children, the following suggestions will apply.

Selecting Books

Use books that are age-appropriate. You will probably use picture books with younger elementary-aged children, but try to avoid titles that have very young characters or that are babyish.

Use books with clear language. It is better to skip books with made-up words that autistic kids might not comprehend, like titles by Dr. Seuss. Also avoid books like the *Amelia Bedelia* series, which is all about idioms, unless you include a lesson about idioms in the program.

Try books about nature and animals. As librarian Heather Baucum notes, the best thing about nature is that you don't have to break down the social cues of a tree! These informational titles are good for discussions and can serve as a lead-in to a fiction book on the same topic.

Use books with clear illustrations. Avoid books with abstract images, or with cluttered spreads or too many colors. Books about things that the children encounter in their own lives are a good choice for concrete thinkers, and photographs or photorealistic illustrations are easier for them to understand than is stylized art or anthropomorphic characters.

Try a picture walk. Try using a "picture walk" rather than a straightforward reading of a fiction picture book. A picture walk is a technique used in schools to help children with reading comprehension use the information provided in a book's illustrations. Picture walks encourage children to observe details in the pictures and relate them to the whole, and they can help many children infer what will happen in the text. To do a picture walk, start with the book's cover. Show the illustration and ask the children what they notice. Move on to the end papers, the title page, and the other pages in the book. Keep your questions concrete. Ask: "What do you think is happening?" rather than "What do you think the character is feeling?" This exercise will help engage the students and give you some idea of the background knowledge they bring to the book.

Try wordless books. A wordless book is a book that tells a story entirely through illustrations. Some wordless picture books can work well in book discussions for early elementary-aged children. As they do in a picture walk, the children can bring their own ideas and backgrounds to help describe the story. Another benefit to using these books is that there are no wrong answers. When you share, go through the wordless book a second time, "reading" the text to the children or telling the story of the book as you see it. This repetition will facilitate comprehension.

Book Discussions for Older Elementary and Middle School Students (Grades 3–8)

Beyond storytimes, older children will enjoy participating in book discussion groups. A book discussion program for older elementary and middle-school students usually involves the librarian selecting a book the children read on their own at home. The book is then discussed at the library.

Types of Books to Discuss

How do you choose the right books for a group that includes autistic children? Although each person is unique, the following guidelines can be a helpful starting point, and will work for all children in the inclusive group.

Choose informational books. Informational books often have an organization and sequence that are easy to follow. These books often provide visual supports (tables, charts, photos, and diagrams), and there is little need to make inferences about what will happen next. While many informational books will appeal to a child, one that relates to their area of interest will have especially strong appeal. Conversely, some types of fiction may present challenges for autistic children, especially when the plot is driven by the internal thoughts, feelings, and desires of the characters. Once past the level of early readers, fiction books offer few visual supports to help with comprehension. And realistic fiction often reflects the social rules of the target audience, so a social situation in a novel might be as confusing to an autistic child or tween as the real-world event would be. On the other hand, you might find that reading and discussing situations in realistic fiction provides your children with powerful opportunities to learn and engage with their peers. This could open up robust conversations and provide opportunities for growth. Every child is different, and every book group is too. You might test the waters with a short piece of realistic fiction to see if it works for your group.

Try fantasy and science fiction. When it comes to works of fiction, autistic readers often enjoy fantasy and science fiction. Fantasy and science fiction create and explain carefully constructed worlds, and the characters tend to have well-defined social roles. There is no assumption that the reader has prior knowledge of how things work, as there is in realistic fiction. There are often stereotyped characters and formulaic plots in these genres that make the stories predictable. Books about superheroes and ones with concrete good vs. evil plots are easy to comprehend and are especially appealing.

Read novels that have neurodivergent characters. Everyone enjoys reading and discussing books about kids they can identify with. Try introducing a title like *Get a Grip, Vivy Cohen,* by Sarah Kapit, to your book club with autistic readers. This title is not only written by an autistic author, but centers on an autistic character—one who is not just a foil to another character's growth. These types of books may be good choices for an inclusive program, as they can provide an entry point for autistic children to explain their experience to their typically developing peers if they choose to have those conversations. Be careful—this is a personal decision, and it should never be initiated by you. More excellent titles like *Get a Grip* are released every year, and some of them are by autistic authors. Do a search online to see what is new since the time of this book's publication. Librarian Adriana White describes the importance of building a collection of books by autistic authors in chapter 7. Flip ahead to read her suggested titles for a variety of age groups.

Ask for input. Ask for input from the autistic children who attend your programs. Some may have favorite books or series they want to introduce to their peers. It is always a good idea to encourage their independence and agency.

Pick books with lots of action. Autistic readers often prefer books that are driven by action, rather than description or character development.

Choose books with visuals. Visual representations of any kind always help readers make sense of people or scenes. For this reason, your school-age readers may enjoy graphic novels, which by definition are highly visual, or heavily illustrated series books such as *Diary of a Wimpy Kid* (2007) and its sequels by Jeff Kinney. When asked to pick a book to read, an autistic child might choose one that has an illustration of the protagonist on the cover because that way they know what the character looks like.

Choose books based on participants' interests. If you have a frequent participant and know that they have a particular interest, you might consider discussing a book about that subject. This will make them feel welcome, and it will allow them to be the expert in the group.

THE IMPORTANCE OF CULTIVATING THE HABIT OF READING PRINT MATERIALS *Charlie Remy*

I hardly read any books for nearly a decade after I graduated from library school because I was filling most of my free time with watching online news videos.

Prior to going on a summer vacation, I decided to try an experiment: *no more news!* I figured I had nothing to lose . . . My plan was to not consume any news whatsoever during this vacation (as someone on the spectrum, my natural inclination to navigating life is with an all or nothing approach). I ended up reading more books during that vacation than I had likely read over the previous year. I started using the local public library regularly for the first time in many years. This positive and intellectually fulfilling activity has helped improve my overall quality of life and emotional well-being.

A core element of this change is reading print books. Despite my role as an electronic resources librarian, I have noticed several benefits from this format: less distraction from multitasking, which can decrease sensory overload; increased attention span; greater relaxation and stress reduction; the materiality involved in holding a book and turning its pages; optimized "sleep hygiene"; and the sense of accomplishment upon noticing physical progression through a book.

Libraries can help cultivate lifelong print reading habits by continuing to feature them as a central component of youth and teen collections and programming. It concerns me somewhat that libraries are increasingly turning their focus and resources away from books onto other initiatives such as video gaming, makerspaces, and other activities. I think some of this is an attempt to maintain relevance in a world dominated by endless use of smartphones and social media. The problem is it can become unbalanced with less emphasis placed on print reading and more on interactive activities centered around technology. I return to the concept of balance here. Youth collections and programs should continue to focus on print reading as an integral part of their mission while also offering innovative collections and services.

A way to encourage youth to read more would be to start with their parents. Consistently modeling intellectual behavior in front of kids can help form lifelong habits. Libraries could consider partnering with Dolly Parton's Imagination Library initiative, which provides enrolled children with one free book per month (https://imaginationlibrary.com/usa).

Going "back to the basics" and reading print books has been such a positive lifestyle change for me. It is a rich antidote to a world with an overabundance of screens and distractions, and the sensory overload that results. Fortunately, our brains offer us the ability to retrain themselves through neuroplasticity—the creation of new pathways which can overwrite long-standing ones. In my case, reading print books has improved my ability to concentrate, decreased levels of stress, and improved my overall quality of life. As a result, I am confident that cultivating autistic kids' print reading habits from an early age will benefit them for the rest of their lives.

One final consideration: reading an e-book might be necessary when a print version is not available (and it's possible that more books might be exclusively electronic in the future). If and when this is the case, kids and young adults could use a dedicated e-book reader or, if using a tablet/smartphone, turn off notifications and close all other apps so they can more effectively focus on the book.

How to Discuss Books with Older Children

Once you've chosen books for the group to read, there are a few more tips that will help make for a more inclusive book club.

Ask concrete questions. As you discuss a book, bear in mind that most autistic children will be better able to answer concrete questions about what is happening in the book, rather than questions that ask them to infer what will happen next or to interpret the feelings or relationships of the characters. When referring to a chapter book the children have read on their own, lead the discussion with simple "wh" questions (who, what, which one, when, and where) and the "h" question (how).

From there, you may choose to move on to more complex, inferential, and abstract questions that are appropriate to the comprehension level of the other attendees. As you ask questions of the group, remember to leave sufficient time for children to process the auditory input before they respond. In your response to a child's comment, include the child's words in your statement, then expand on it, introducing your own ideas.

Use props and fidgets. Social rules guide group interactions, and it is these social rules that can be tough to navigate for autistic children. They can be baffled by the unspoken rules we follow that let us know when it is our turn to speak in a group, what is appropriate to say, and when we need to listen to others. Having an object that is passed to a child when it is their turn to speak can help with these issues during a program. In addition to giving each child a tangible reminder of when it is or is not their turn to speak, the object can also serve as a calming fidget item if the child holding it experiences anxiety about speaking in front of the group.

If you are discussing an informational book, in addition to a turn-taking object, you can try using a prop such as reading comprehension cubes to facilitate the discussion. There are a number of these on the market, and they are inexpensive. The cubes are imprinted with comprehension questions such as: "What happened in the story?" and "How was a problem solved?" The child throws the cube and tries to answer the question that is on its top surface. To avoid putting a child on the spot, others in the group can join in and assist with the answer, or you can provide cues and hints from the reading to help the child come up with an answer on their own. You can also make comprehension cubes using free templates; try searching "reading comprehension cubes" online for both free templates and cubes available for purchase. Or you can make a simple comprehension tool by writing questions with a permanent marker on sections of an inflated beach ball. Throw the ball to a child and see if they can answer the question their hand touches when they catch it.

Other Program Ideas

Beyond book discussions, there are many ways you can provide excellent programming for school-age autistic children. Here are just a few other programs to try that might appeal to the autistic children you work with.

Dog Therapy

In collaboration with a local animal-assisted therapy group, the Skokie (IL) Public Library offers a successful dog therapy program for older children. Librarian Holly Jin notes that the success of this program is based on the skill and commitment of the dog handlers the library collaborates with, as well as the parents' commitment and connection. Parents are asked to wait in the lobby while their children work with the dogs; part of the session involves children walking the dogs through the lobby, which gives families a chance to connect and take pictures during the program. Each session is an hour long, and children are matched individually with a dog at the start of the session. Together with their dogs, the children work through activities such as modified bowling, setting up a treat for the dogs under each pin. This engages fine motor skills, and allows kids to give commands, which works on verbal skills.

MAKE IT VIRTUAL Jin's dog therapy program has thrived in the online environment as well. Children and dog handlers log in to a web-conferencing software synchronously; then the children and dogs are matched up and meet in pairs or small groups in breakout rooms. The dogs are trained to hit a button in response to questions, and the kids enjoy asking "yes or no" questions to their dogs. Additionally, the dogs are trained to pull emoji-stuffed toys from a bag. The dog handlers use these as cues; for example: "Sophie pulled out a crying face; she must be feeling sad today. Do you know why she might feel sad? Have you ever felt sad?"

Yoga

Yoga is an ancient practice that has gone in and out of fashion in the United States over the past few decades. It is now very popular, and it is likely that many librarians reading this are yoga practitioners. Yoga is not only great for librarians and other adults, but it is also wonderful for kids, and it has many sensory integration benefits for autistic children. If you do yoga, it is not too big a stretch for you to consider leading a yoga program that includes autistic kids.

MAKE IT VIRTUAL
You can stream your yoga sessions online and allow children and their parents or caregivers to join in virtually. Look around: there may well be someone in your area who would be happy to conduct a program for you.

There are many books and websites that show yoga postures for children that you can incorporate into your program. The following resources specifically address doing yoga with autistic children:

- *Yoga Journal* has a series of guided yoga videos. Search their website (www.yogajournal.com) for "autism."
- *Yoga for Children and Young People with Autism*, by Michael Chissick (2019)

If you have iPads in your library, try using a yoga app to guide your activities. You can also use a deck of yoga cards with illustrated postures to provide a visual aid during the program. If you don't feel comfortable leading the program yourself, see if there is a yoga instructor from the community who would like to lead the session.

YOGA, MINDFULNESS, AND PROGRAM GUIDELINES
Charlie Remy

I have been intermittently practicing yoga for the past five years, and I cannot remember a time when I regretted it as the benefits become clearly evident. I feel more confident (especially when I realize that my body is capable of yoga postures I initially thought were not possible for me), and yoga improves gross motor skills/balance/stamina, quiets the mind, and allows for socializing with others during the same activity.

Providing free classes at the library could make yoga more accessible to people from lower incomes as studios can be quite costly. In addition to removing economic barriers, this kind of initiative would get kids moving and away from their electronic devices. Integrating mindfulness and breath work could reduce their anxiety levels and give them tools to better cope with the stressors of life.

Numerous varieties of yoga exist (fast/slow, heated, many props/minimal props, background music/silence, etc.), and teachers in these contexts need to be aware of the potential for sensory overload. For example, in my own experience, I cannot practice heated *vinyasa* yoga. The ninety-degree heat would be highly unpleasant, and I would be unable to mentally and physically process the teacher's rapid flow of instructions. When I am unable to comprehend yoga instructions, I tend to give up on all subsequent poses and become frustrated and embarrassed with myself for not being able to keep up with the rest of the class.

I have found that yin and restorative yoga are a good fit for my learning style and challenges with gross motor skills, stability, and strength. The slower pace of these practices helps students focus on breath and calming the mind. I would suggest that the teacher begin with no background music, and then once students are more accustomed to the poses after several sessions, ask them if some soft music without lyrics could be added. Lyrics could prevent students from effectively receiving the teacher's instructions. Classes should be small (ideally no more than five students) in a quiet room with plenty of space. Fast-paced practices with complicated flows like *vinyasas* should be avoided.

The teaching style matters significantly as it could encourage students to attend more classes or, conversely, make the class so inaccessible that they give up and never return. Patience is key. Providing slow, clear instructions and repeating them more than once is helpful. Continuous demonstration of the poses in front of the class can give students a clear example of the correct alignment. Do not assume that the students have memorized the pose even after several repetitions. It may be effective to have one teacher giving the instructions and providing an example at the front of the class and another teacher walking around the room to provide constructive feedback to students. Personally, I appreciate reassurance from the teacher that I am doing the pose correctly or specific suggestions on how to improve, particularly when I first learn it. This reassurance builds my self-confidence.

Free, high-quality yoga classes attuned to autistic needs would be a good addition to school and public library services for kids and young adults. The benefits could be numerous: increased biomechanical self-awareness and confidence, stress reduction, more opportunities to socialize while doing a common activity, and a better balance between physical and intellectual activities. Kids who begin to learn about the possibilities of yoga practice from an early age could cultivate a positive and proactive lifelong activity.

Drop-in Gaming

Whether you play video games or tabletop games, gaming is fun for all ages. Use the games that you have to set up stations in your meeting or children's room, and let the children have fun. Place a game at each table, and make sure the rules are visible. Board games like checkers and Sorry, and card games such as Uno work well for this age group. You can also simplify the rules and provide a visual schedule to offer more support. Try to avoid games that require social interpretation, such as Apples to Apples. If you have a video game setup, be sure to regulate the volume. Though a drop-in gaming session will largely run itself, as with all children's programs, be prepared to step in to provide support and behavioral guidance if needed.

MAKE IT VIRTUAL Gaming programs can easily be hosted online. You may think that only video games can be played virtually, but some traditional tabletop games have online versions that actually work just as well as the in-person games. You can purchase the online edition of Monopoly, for example, for about the same price as the physical game, and then invite participants to join you virtually. Games such as Uno and Rummikub are also available to play online. You can explore online for some of your kids' favorites to see what options you have.

DUNGEONS & DRAGONS PROGRAMS ALIGN WITH LIBRARIANSHIP CORE VALUES   *Karen Kinsey*

Best practices when programming and meeting the needs of people on the autism spectrum include limiting enrollment and controlling the environment. Limiting the enrollment allows for more individual support and reduces sensory distractions. The use of teen or adult assistants is also advantageous. One example of such a program is Dungeons & Dragons for middle-school students. I currently work with a school librarian whose thirteen-year-old son is autistic. He is going to lead a Dungeons & Dragons pop-up class at our middle school. While he might be the only participant who is autistic in this specific program, this program would be ideal for a group of students on the autism spectrum or a mixed group of students. Her son is both an authority on the game, as well as sensitive to the needs of students and youth on the autism spectrum.

This program can be offered weekly, bimonthly, or monthly. It can also be run simultaneously with other programs for younger siblings, and adult support/educational programs. Dungeons & Dragons, for example, can be held in the library, at a school or community building, or during an existing meeting/program for people on the autism spectrum and their families. This could also apply to other groups with disabilities. Again, limiting enrollment and controlling the environment ensure best practices.

In order to follow ALA guidelines, values, and best practices, it is essential to consider the needs of the patrons being served. Offering programs and services that enrich the social and emotional learning of the community trumps reaching attendance and participation numbers.

STEM Programs

Librarian Erin Lovelace notes that many of the autistic children in her library have a really targeted interest, and a lot of times that interest is in science. One of the most popular programs she hosted for older kids was a "deconstruction" program, in which they brought in old or broken toys and the kids took them apart carefully, examining the inner workings as they deconstructed them. Lovelace found that her autistic kids particularly enjoyed participating in this inclusive program. You can find inexpensive items to deconstruct at yard sales and thrift shops, or even at home if you have children of your own. For children with an artistic proclivity, try reconstructing the pieces in a later program to make found-object art projects.

The following sections describe two innovative programs: a LEGO building program, and a program in which the kids make "accidental art."

LEGO BUILDER'S CLUB

Nova Southeastern University, Davie, Florida
Designed by librarians Anne Leon and Meagan Albright;
adapted from a Center for Autism and Related Disorders (CARD) program
for Public Library Services at the Alvin Sherman Library

Frequency: Two hours long, monthly on a Saturday afternoon

Registration: None needed, but limited to a maximum of 20 participants

Ages: 6 and up

Many autistic children enjoy building with LEGOs or similar toy products. Some like to build the kits that come with detailed instructions and produce one object, while others like to just put the blocks together in random ways, or create something they design themselves. A number of libraries offer LEGO building programs that are appropriate for these children. The Alvin Sherman Library's program is one example. One librarian leads the program with the assistance of teen volunteers. Parents don't have to stay in the room, but they are required to stay in the Public Library Services Department. LEGO Builder's Club is an inclusive program, for ages six and up, that meets monthly on a Saturday afternoon.

What You'll Need

- Tables for the LEGOs
- LEGO building bases (optional)
- Basic LEGO blocks (you can purchase some and ask library users to donate some)
- Digital camera

Room Setup

Configure the tables into social groups, depending on the kids who drop in on any given day. For big construction projects, the floor can be divided into zones with masking tape. Adjust the overhead lighting to the comfort level of the participants.

SAMPLE PROGRAM PLAN

The LEGO Builder's Club is unstructured. Essentially, the library provides the space and the materials and lets the children build on their own. The librarian circulates, helping children with ideas, offering praise, and providing transition reminders when the end of the club period is approaching. The librarian can also use the digital camera to record the participants' creations. These can be e-mailed to the club members or used in library materials (remember to get the parents' permission to use the images).

BEAUTIFUL OOPS! MAKING ACCIDENTAL ART

Designed by art educators Michelle López, Jennifer Candiano, and Hana Joo; adapted from a program at the Queens Library and Queens Museum of Art, New York City

Frequency: One hour each week for six weeks

Ages: 5–12

Working together, the Queens Library and the Queens Museum of Art created this program series based on the book *Beautiful Oops! Making Accidental Art* by Barney Saltzberg (2010). This book shows how accidents like spills can be turned into beautiful art. A librarian and a support staff person co-lead the program. Parents are asked to stay in the room to support and prompt their children and to manage their behavior.

What You'll Need

- A visual schedule
- Two rows of tables
- Brown butcher paper to cover tables
- Materials for art projects (each session needs glue sticks, scissors, markers, crayons, and construction paper). Other materials may be needed based on the theme.
- Visual vocabulary sheets
- Baskets for the art supplies and paper to label the contents
- A checklist with the steps in the art project
- Turn-taking object
- A selection of art-themed picture books
- Small prize items such as stickers or small gifts
- Certificates for participants

SAMPLE PROGRAM PLAN

Room Setup

Cover the tabletops with butcher paper, and arrange the tables in two rows facing each other, with space in between. With this arrangement the children can see each other and take advantage of social opportunities, and the librarians can walk between the tables to supervise and engage the children. Arrange the materials on another table as a "buffet." Use baskets to sort the types of materials, and label each basket so children will be encouraged to ask for items by name. Invite the children to explore the materials.

Introductory Art Activity

Use drawing or coloring to warm the children up for making art and to keep the participants involved while waiting. Provide paper, markers, or crayons and art-themed picture books for ideas.

Welcome

Sing the same hello song each time. Introduce or review the visual schedule, which shows what the group will do each week. Ask each child to introduce himself, passing around a turn-taking prop.

INTRODUCE THE WEEKLY THEME

Use a visual vocabulary, like the one shown in figure 5.1. Then show an excerpt from *Beautiful Oops!* Explain and reinforce the idea of turning mistakes into art that has the week's theme. (See below for details.)

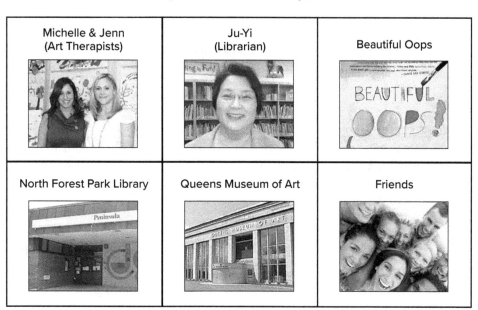

FIGURE 5.1 Visual vocabulary

Portion of visual vocabulary used by the Queens (NY) partnership

Art Making

With the parents' assistance, move the children through the steps of the art project. (See the details below.) Have checklists available to help with the sequence of steps.

Transition

Verbally warn the children when they have five minutes, and then one minute, left for the activity.

Cleanup

Ask the children to clean up their area of the table and help with putting away materials. Assign specific tasks to each child and give very clear directions. After cleanup, reward each child with a small prize to take home. This can be a sticker, hand stamp, or an inexpensive toy.

Round Up and Share

Invite the children to display their work on a table at the front of the room and have everyone look at all of the artwork. Give each participant a chance to express pride in their work. Ask the children to say a nice thing about someone else's work.

Goodbye

Encourage the children to say goodbye to each other.

WEEKLY THEMES AND MATERIALS

Ripping

Children rip up newspaper and tissue paper and glue the pieces to cover cardboard boxes or Styrofoam balls.

Stains

Children stain watercolor paper with items like flavored teas, Kool-Aid, fruit juice, coffee, or chocolate. Use the caps from old markers instead of paintbrushes to spread the stains. If the items have a scent, have the students smell them before making the stains.

Spills

Show the children how to use eyedroppers to spill liquids on watercolor paper, and use paintbrushes to spread the spills. Markers can be used to outline images in the art, and glitter and sequins can be pasted on to enhance the artwork.

Smudges

Give the children oil pastels and blending sticks to make smudged art. Other items like markers can enhance the projects.

Holes

Provide a number of differently shaped hole-punches from a crafts store and have the children punch holes in paper; then decorate the sheets by gluing on the cutouts and using markers or embellishments.

Bubble Art

Invite the children to blow bubbles as a group (with the bubble mixture colored with food coloring) onto white paper. Once the bubble stains dry on the paper, the children can use markers to outline pictures they see in the bubbles.

At the end of the last meeting, give each child a certificate commending them for their good work.

Gardening

Gardening is a sensory-rich activity, teaches kids about food, and allows them to work on a number of skills, including math. Shelley Harris, a children's librarian at the Oak Park (IL) Public Library, hosts what she describes as "Supported Gardening" programs for kids with disabilities, their families, and friends. Gardening provides a space where children feel a sense of ownership and can take a leadership role. To make her gardening programs accessible, Harris has the following supports available:

- Easi-Grip garden tools
- Gloves
- Lightweight, Easi-Grip watering cans with a rain shower spout
- Kneeling pads
- A bench for sitting
- Augmentative and alternative communication (AAC) boards showing pictures and words related to gardening. Harris also has a permanently placed AAC picture board welcoming visitors to the garden.

FIGURE 5.2

Augmentative and alternative communication (AAC) board and materials

AAC board and materials at the Oak Park Public Library

You don't have to be a master gardener to get a garden set up with your kids. Harris started with no experience, and asked for help from community and programming partners. Some of the plants they've had success with are:

- Snapdragons: fun to play with, and they snap
- Succulents: easy to care for
- False indigo: has a nice rattle in the wind
- Prairie sock: tall with sandpaper-like leaves
- Nasturtium: high success rate and edible peppery flowers
- Kale: turns green to purple as the weather cools, and is edible
- Lamb's ear: great soft texture; plant it next to kale for different texture contrasts
- Dragon's breath: has a soft leathery feel and is bright red
- Daffodils: plant in the fall, and it's a lot of fun to watch them bloom in the spring

Most recently, Harris partnered with a high school class to build wheelchair-accessible raised garden beds, in which children have planted herbs. The herb gardening programs have now grown into companion cooking programs—the herbs are harvested during every session and used in recipes like salsa, dips, and mint lemonade with basic 2−6-step visual recipes (but be aware of any allergies before eating these creations; some libraries might also require a signed waiver before serving children food). Note that mint and lemon mint are invasive plants, so be sure to plant these in container gardens.

One of Harris's favorite things about gardening programs is that there are so many ways to participate, and no wrong one. If children don't want to touch dirt or plants, they can document everything by taking photos. Or they are welcome to grab a book and sit in the garden and read. Any size space can work; a garden can be built in raised beds, containers by the front door, or on a patio.

Carrie Banks, head of the Brooklyn Public Library's Inclusive Services, has provided inclusive gardening since 1999 and can attest to its benefits for all children. Particularly in an urban setting such as hers, no child has an advantage, as everyone is new to gardening. As Banks says, "This is worth a lot. With some other activities, especially those on academic calendars, kids without disabilities may have more experience. But these are city kids, and no one knows anything about growing plants."[1] Her favorite gardening activity with kids is planting tomatoes, peppers, and onions, as they show up in so many cuisines.

Banks suggests the following tips for creating inclusive gardening spaces and programs:

- Have children work in pairs or groups to support and learn from each other.
- Allow flexibility in timing, and let children take projects home if they aren't finished.
- Utilize and train volunteers, particularly those with disabilities, to work one-on-one with children when needed. Children need role models.
- Support communication with AAC. Banks uses a variety of AAC, including sign language, Mayer-Johnson symbols, and Spanish. She uses Boardmaker with Mayer-Johnson symbols since Brooklyn schools use them.
- Create a social narrative so children know what to expect and can prepare.
- Use a visual schedule so children know what comes next and won't get anxious.
- Incorporate music. It's fun and supports learning for some youth.
- Make sure all tools and plants are child safe, and only use natural pest control methods. Supervise the children closely, and provide sun protection and non-latex gloves.

Video Sharing

Designed by librarian Kate Thompson, this program provides an opportunity for sharing one's interests and developing public speaking skills. While we're introducing it here, it could also easily be used with teens.

As Thompson says, "one characteristic of autism is the tendency to have strong interests in particular subjects. This leads to students who are natural experts in their chosen area of expertise. This interest in focused research on a topic makes the students' own interests a natural fit with the library's staff and resources. By allowing students to share their interests with each other, we can achieve several goals:

- Give students an opportunity to share their interest and practice presentation skills.
- Provide students with topics for conversation with each other and exposure to new interests.
- Give librarians concrete examples with which to demonstrate the library's resources, collection, and utility."

VIDEO SHARING PROGRAM

Designed by librarian Kate Thompson

Ages: Older children and/or teens

Advertise this program in advance and have students send you links to their video selections. This allows you to be the conduit for the videos and make the final decision on what gets shown and is appropriate for the group. Have a time limit on the length of the videos, keeping in mind that it will take a few minutes to set up and introduce each video. Create a YouTube playlist of the videos, and consider using a website sure as ViewPure to play the videos without advertisements.

Once you've received the list of videos, you can look in the library's collection for related materials to have on display and available for checkout. Think creatively about what you want to display, and choose a selection from a variety of media. For example, a video involving weather phenomena could lead to a display that includes a book and CD set of Judi Barrett's *Cloudy with a Chance of Meatballs,* as well as nonfiction selections. Be sure to demonstrate items from the library's e-book, audiobook, and related digital services as well. Display the items attractively on a table at the back of the room, so that students may get up and look at them during the program.

What You'll Need
- A quiet space with minimal distraction and comfortable seating
- A laptop with HDMI cable
- A projector
- A video you've chosen as a demonstration
- Books and resources from your library's collection
- Fidget items
- A visual schedule
- A printout of topics/links (optional)

SAMPLE PROGRAM PLAN

WELCOME

Greet students at the library entrance or have clearly marked signage pointing to the room. Introduce yourself and any other staff members.

Introduce the visual schedule. This could be on a projector or as simple as a list on a whiteboard. It should include each step of the program with a simple illustration. For example:

- Hello (person waving)
- Videos (picture of TV screen)
- Browse Books (picture of books)
- Say Goodbye (hand waving)

Room Setup

Be sure to address the physical space, pointing out bathroom locations and the quiet room (if available), as well as expectations for behavior. It can be reassuring to state that you do not expect silence and that everyone is encouraged to share their thoughts about the program as it goes along.

VIDEO SHARING

Demonstrate video sharing by introducing your own video, describing why you picked it and what you like about it. Share the order of presentations and write down the names in order somewhere visible. Ask each student to introduce their video as it is played.

In the last ten minutes or so, introduce the table of materials that you've pulled from the library's collection and allow students to browse the items. If time allows, you could also demonstrate some of the library's digital resources on the projection screen (how to check out e-books, access databases, etc.).

You may want to have prepared a handout that describes some of the subjects from the videos and has additional resources or links to the video that was shared, so that students can learn more on their own and have a souvenir of the event.

GOODBYE

Thank everyone for coming. Encourage them to seek assistance from the library staff in digging deeper on the topics touched upon in the videos.

Programs to Supplement Schoolwork

You can work with the special education classrooms in your community to find ways to supplement school-age children's educational experiences through your own programming. Find out what they are learning about, and provide programming that ties in with these themes. For example, librarian Renee Grassi learned that a group of students was learning about manners at their school, so she developed a program on that topic for her public library. Not only did this program supplement their schoolwork, but it also provided them with an opportunity to practice a set of life skills in a real-world setting. And as a bonus, the program helped familiarize these students with the library and with strategies for finding and accessing library resources.

Teachers will also be able to share with you any special interests that members of their group have that are not school-related, such as Pokémon, superheroes, or Harry Potter, and you can develop programs that speak to those interests and are fun and engaging for autistic children.

MANNERS

Developed by Renee Grassi

Time needed: One hour

For this program to be successful, front-desk staff must feel comfortable interacting with autistic teens. Be sure to prepare the staff who will be working that day by giving them a basic "About Autism" overview. (See the training resources in "Appendix A: Training and Education" for a good starting point.)

What You'll Need
- Visual schedule
- A ball or fidget for passing around the circle
- Books to read aloud about manners

SAMPLE PROGRAM PLAN

BEFORE THE PROGRAM
- Work with the teacher to have teens prepare a notecard they will bring with them to the library. On the notecard, they should write down a question they have for a librarian.
- Make sure that staff are prepared and comfortable for the interaction. This includes ensuring they are knowledgeable about autism; and reviewing the program with them so they know what to expect.
- Set up a meeting room or other designated space with a visual schedule and prepare an agenda.
- Create the visual schedule.

AT THE PROGRAM

Welcome
Welcome teens to the program and review the visual schedule together.

Book
Read a few stories about manners; easy nonfiction picture books work well. Talk about the words used and the situations that arise in these stories.

Activities
- Practice manners. Try passing a ball in a circle (the ball can also double as a fidget). Using a script, the teen holding the ball practices turning to their classmates, saying hello, greeting them, using their names, and then asking a question using good manners.
- Each teen takes their notecard up to the front desk to ask the librarian their question. This allows them to practice and utilize some of the things

they just discussed in the program in a public place. It also allows them to gain knowledge and experience about how to use the library.

AFTER THE PROGRAM

Have a group check-in with the librarians after the program is over to determine what worked and what they have questions about, in order to prepare for next time.

Summer Reading Programs: Inclusive Practices

Summer reading programs, which typically consist of a reading club and dynamic presenters, are a key element of the programming year for every public library. Here we describe ways to ensure that all children, including those who are autistic, will have equal access for participation.

Summer Reading Clubs

There are a number of things you can do to make your summer reading club more inclusive.

Bend the rules a bit to allow for the preferences of autistic children. This might involve letting an autistic child read the same book several times over the course of the summer and get club credit for each reading. The Iowa City Libraries offers this as an option, with great success. Other strategies that they have found to be successful include offering audiobooks instead of written text, and allowing books and materials that are more suited to ability than to age.

Consider accepting other activities in lieu of reading for club participation, like going to a museum, or exploring in nature. Some libraries do this for everyone. An example is Summer Stride at the San Francisco Public Library, which is promoted as a program for all ages and abilities. Their goal is for participants to complete twenty hours of learning during the summer.

Keep a small supply of alternative incentives that would be appropriate for autistic children. Inexpensive fidget items are always a good idea. Modifying or eliminating book-reporting requirements if your library has those may make it easier for autistic children to participate. Instead of a report or a book review, you can ask a couple of simple content questions (not interpretive ones) like "What is the name of the main character?"

Summer Reading Events

There are some things you can do to make even the largest summer reading event more accessible for autistic children. One is to designate a quiet space at the event, and communicate through an announcement and written signage where this space is. Make sure families and children know they can access the space at any time. The Alvin Sherman Library hosts a huge event every year, Storyfest, that brings in crowds of up to 5,000 people. Library Director Anne Leon describes it as a busy, multisensory day. To ensure autistic children can attend, they set up a clearly marked quiet room where families can decompress from the crowd and take time out from the noisy, bustling environment for as much time as they need. You should also consider developing a Social Story that explains what to expect at the event, and post this on the library's website. This will make the event a bit more predictable for the autistic children in your community.

MAKE IT VIRTUAL There are existing online summer reading clubs that you can purchase, and your library may already be using one of these, or you can design your own. In either case, if you offer your reading club online, it can easily be inclusive. Autistic children may feel more comfortable checking into the club and reporting on their reading from the controlled environment of their home. If they need to come to the library to pick up prizes, they can do so when the library tends to be less busy. Children who are not autistic but who have a hard time getting to the physical library building will also benefit from this option. Since some children don't have reliable internet access at home or the proper devices to access it, you might be able to lend iPads, laptops, and hotspots to help remedy some of these issues, or offer a hybrid club with in-library and virtual options. You can also record and livestream your kickoff finale and the presenters in order to allow for virtual attendance at your summer reading club events. Be sure to give children and their families the option to watch live so that they feel like they're part of the action, or to view later. Use chat and other features of your platform to build in participation so that children can engage during a livestream.

Summer Reading Programs: Alternative Events

Ideally, you should design your regular summer programming to be inclusive for children of all abilities. But even if you do, there still might be barriers for some of your autistic school-age children. Perhaps the biggest barrier to participation in summer reading for autistic children is the crowd factor. Public libraries tend to be very busy and noisy places during the summer vacation period, and summer reading events can be chaotic. Great turnout and active participation are extremely positive for libraries, but these environmental factors can make an autistic child very anxious and can lead to a meltdown. We mentioned above a few things you can do to mitigate these conditions. Or you can offer alternatives that will make it easier for these children and their families to participate in summer reading:

Have an after-hours kickoff or finale event. Provide an alternative kickoff or end-of-summer event. Holding the event after the library closes allows staff to control the light and noise levels and make the event more comfortable for the kids with sensory sensitivities. You should limit the number of attendees, but plan to include at these events all of the activities you would have at the standard kickoff or finale to ensure that all kids have access to the same experience.

Host a sensory-friendly version of events. Librarian Renee Grassi brought zoo animals to the library with a conga drum line, but she realized that while the participants enjoyed the animals and music, the whole scene could be "too much" for autistic children. Providing the same experience but with a smaller crowd has proven very successful. She recommends having families register in advance to keep the group to a manageable size and avoid chaos and excessive noise.

Take the library on the road. If your library has a bookmobile, consider using it to bring summer reading programs to your children's neighborhoods. In Iowa City, the Antelope Lending Library makes special bookmobile "sensory stops" every week in August to provide autistic children with a less chaotic environment in which to experience the library.[2] For children who are sensitive to sensory stimulation such as lights, noise, and crowds, these stops allow for a less overwhelming experience. The "sensory stops" also provide outdoor activities adjacent to the bookmobile, so children can participate in creating crafts and other sensory activities, such as playing with kinetic sand. You can incorporate your summer reading program theme into these bookmobile stops, and bring a condensed version of summer reading activities to children who prefer not to come into the library's physical building.

Final Thoughts

School-age children are often considered during planning for summer reading programs and events. While this is a great time to provide programming, don't forget to offer inclusive services and programs throughout the school year too. Many autistic children who have aged out of storytime will benefit from the learning and social opportunities your library can provide all year long.

NOTES

1. Kids Gardening, "Designing Gardening Programs for All," 2016, https://kidsgardening.org/create-sustain-a-program-designing-garden-programs-for-all.

2. Erin Jordan, "Bookmobile Stop Caters to Autistic Children in Iowa City," The Gazette, July 4, 2017, www.thegazette.com/subject/news/bookmobile-stop-caters-to-autistic-children-in-iowa-city-20170704.

Programming
for Teens

ANYONE WHO HAS EVER LIVED OR WORKED WITH A TEENAGER KNOWS that the teen years can be turbulent, often characterized by raging hormones, rebellion, and inconsistent behavior. Teens are engaged in the developmental task of separating from their parents, and for most of them peer relationships become primary as they begin to define what they value and who they will be as adults.

All teens undergo the physiological processes of adolescence. Autistic teens, however, have an additional layer of neuro-complexity to navigate in addition to the physical changes. Differences in communication styles and social understanding can have unintended consequences for them because teens aren't always forgiving of their peers' social missteps. Despite having the same needs as any other teen for companionship and to fit in with their peers, these communication and social differences can lead to autistic teens feeling socially isolated, and sometimes even to their being intentionally targeted or bullied.

Both school and public libraries can be part of the solution for autistic teens by offering programs that give them a chance to socialize and develop friendships, practice life skills, and become engaged in the community in a safe space. Because state-provided autism services end for them at age 21 or 22 and they age out of many school activities and therapies previously available to them, they will have few other avenues for continued learning or community involvement. Their opportunities increase if they can have these social experiences and learn these life skills while they're still students.

Whenever possible, you should provide inclusive programming that is welcoming for all teens. After all, when you're a teen, there's nothing worse than not fitting in. Targeted programs for this age group of autistics can actually make things harder for them by requiring them to differentiate themselves from their peers. The programs also keep teens from interactions and forging connections with their neurotypical peers, experiences that can benefit them as they move out of school into the adult world. That being said, every person is different, and some teens need more specialized, individual support. For these teens, autism-specific programming may be more appropriate. As always, it is important to assess your own community and be flexible in adapting to the needs of the individuals and families you serve. In this chapter we will introduce ideas for inclusive programming, providing examples of programs in which many autistic teens will feel comfortable, even those with higher support needs. We will also explore teen volunteering opportunities, as well as ideas for teens who would benefit from more supportive programs.

Inclusive Teen Programming Ideas

Since the programs introduced in this section work well with many teens, it's possible you are already implementing variations of at least some of them. And because these programs might have particular appeal for autistic teens, it is especially important if you hold them that you make them accessible and inclusive. Regardless of what types of programs you offer for teens, we always suggest having snacks available. You'll likely find that more teens want to come to a program when pizza or chips are involved; this also gives them another opportunity to engage with each other while grazing. Make sure that some food choices are available for teens with food allergies or aversions.

Take a look at the following ideas—these are programs that can be modified to fit nearly every public library. If you get stumped as you're trying to figure out how best to make one apply to your environment, reach out to your local community stakeholders to ask what would suit their needs.

STEM Programs

For many years Erin Lovelace, a children's librarian at the Henrico County (VA) Public Library, has helped to run a sensory storytime for younger autistic children. She noticed that many of the autistic teens who grew up in her library are attracted to its inclusive STEM or science programs for teens. As she noted, a lot of her autistic kids have a really targeted interest, and many times that interest is science-related.

MAKE IT VIRTUAL
Many STEM programs lend themselves easily to the virtual environment. For example, you can invite your coding club to meet online, using Zoom or another platform that has chat and breakout rooms.

Studies have confirmed this connection. Results from the National Longitudinal Transition Study-2 (NLTS-2) indicate that autistic college students are more likely to pursue degrees in STEM than in any other field of studies.[1] You can help these teens dig deeper into their interests or explore new areas in STEM by providing creative programming for them. There are so many good examples of STEM programming for teens, including computer coding classes, LEGO events, and low-tech building projects. Try filtering programs by "STEM" on the Teen

Services Underground website (www.teenservicesunderground.com), or browse through the many ideas listed on the STEM in Libraries website (www.stemin libraries.com) for inspiration.

Crafting

Craft programs in libraries are popular with all ages, and teens are no exception. You might already have programs like this in place since teens love to work with their hands to create. Autistic teens might particularly benefit from craft programs that help them practice and develop fine motor skills. Go beyond the holiday-related crafts that are commonly offered to people with disabilities. Instead, offer the opportunity to make things that have more teen appeal, like tie-dyeing clothes or making jewelry from hardware. Duct tape crafts are always popular with teens, especially the duct tape wallet. Try building a program around constructing duct tape wallets, and build in a quick financial literacy lesson while the teens are crafting.

Creative Writing

Holly Jin of the Skokie (IL) Public Library has noticed that many autistic teens are drawn to her library's writing programs. You can replicate her success by offering creative writing and poetry workshops for the autistic teens in your community. All teens need a way to share their thoughts and feelings through creative outlets, and libraries can provide them with the time and space to do so. While teens should be allowed to get creative and express themselves however they wish, be sure to provide some structure to the program for those teens who need it. Offer a brief lesson or some suggested guidelines that could be followed before setting teens off on their own to create, and provide some examples. If teens are willing to share, you might host a showcase of their works. This could be done by posting their work on the physical walls of the library, or by posting it online in the library's virtual environment. Retired librarian Paul Wyss was inspired to create poetry as a young adult after taking a college course; introducing these ideas to teens at a younger age might allow them to express themselves in ways that are otherwise unavailable to them.

MAKE IT VIRTUAL
Creative writing groups can not only meet online, but the work created in them can also be presented through a virtual showcase. Hold a virtual kickoff event through a live online session, and post creative writings on your library's website or social media channels.

CREATIVE WRITING
Paul Wyss

I've been very lucky in life. As a first-year student in college, I was fortunate to have poet Tom McKeown for my English 101 professor. Tom authored *The Luminous Revolver* (among other works) and taught me a great deal about writing. He also had a strong influence on my writing of poetry. Writing, in any form, tells a story. I have written successfully academically, and now I will be returning to the practice of writing poems and song lyrics.

"The Moon" was an acknowledgment that I was having difficulty living. I was never comfortable in life. This was before my Asperger's diagnosis, and I felt as though something was haunting me. I felt as though something was always with me.

The Moon

I can see the sun behind the moon; not the moon behind the sun.
Trivial, it seems.
Fundamental, it is.
On its diurnal round a pale visitor passes: its gravity strong and silent.
In my mirror, surrounded by a shroud of ice, I see its true luminance.
It passes as my eyes close.
I wake and it is gone until the sun sets again and crystals form in the sky like the tears of a veiled bride.
It passes from blue to white to black.
In slivers, fragments, and ovals, it fashions its image in a shadow.

"Woodlawn" came about as I was walking on Woodlawn Avenue in Bloomington, Indiana. I was returning to my apartment from "leg day" at the YMCA, and I was wondering why no one understood me. Well, I guess it's difficult to understand someone with Asperger's. Still, I was fortunate to chronicle these thoughts in a poem.

Woodlawn

I walk alone,
wearing a pauper's coat,
holding twenty-six letters and eight notes—
all that I need to truly be me.
I can spell a word and write a sentence to paint a picture.
I can count to four, and sometimes even twelve,
and then touch ivory, maple or steel, and make a sound.
All that I am—
all that I will be—
wrapped up in what I can do with a pen, paper, and my hands.
It's all so simple,
and no one can see it,
and so I walk on Woodlawn.

> Writing is therapeutic. I would encourage everyone to write—it helps to clarify thoughts and emotions. Not everyone has to be Sylvia Plath or William Carlos Williams to be an effective writer. Sometimes, writing for one's self is enough.

Gaming

We mentioned gaming as a program idea for school-age children; not surprisingly, these programs are also popular with teens. Offering gaming at the library has the advantage of putting the experience in a social context, and giving autistic gamers an opportunity to connect, relieve stress, and immerse themselves in an enjoyable pastime.[2] A gaming program or series of programs may be just the thing to get all teens into the library, and could be especially appealing for autistic teens.

There is a strong community of autistic gamers, and you might find that the ones in your area are already meeting to game together. Do a quick search online, or look at meetup.com, to see if there are any gaming groups in your community that you can invite in to use the library's space. They might be surprised to learn that they can game for free at the library.

While you might think "video game" when seeing the word gaming, low-tech tabletop gaming programs can be just as enjoyable—and are much more cost-effective for libraries on a budget. The Albert Wisner Public Library in New York state implemented a successful low-tech game night for autistic teens. They set up tables with a variety of games that have low barriers to entry, such as Uno, Connect 4, and Jenga, as well as life-size games that allow for more physical movement. They started the program with "Getting to Know You" Bingo, which helped participants feel comfortable with one another in the room. While this was designed as a targeted program, it could be equally appealing to all teens in an inclusive group. Consider adding some newer popular games like Ticket to Ride to the classic board games you make available for teens to play. You might also modify the rules and simplify instructions to make the games easier to follow.

MAKE IT VIRTUAL Many low-tech games can be played online with all participants logged on to the same virtual meeting software such as Zoom. Teens can still socialize with one another while attending from their own homes. Scattergories is one example that's available online.* Try searching to see if your teens' favorite games can also be played remotely.

*www.teenlibrarian\toolbox.com/2020/05/tween-and-teen-programming-ideas-online-scattergories-is-the-word-game-you-need

GAMING AND THE AUTISTIC
GAMING INITIATIVE (AGI)

Steph Diorio

If my parents hadn't bought my brother and I a Nintendo 64 and Banjo-Kazooie when I was in fourth grade, I would be a very different person.

My name is Steph, and I wasn't diagnosed with autism until I was twenty years old. (Hi, Steph!) I was born in 1989, and autistic girls weren't exactly talked about much during the 1990s and 2000s, so I flew under the radar.

Had I been diagnosed a lot earlier, a lot of things would have been very different for me. The services I would've had access to would have been lacking compared to what we have today, but I definitely would have benefited from social skills training. In middle school, I went through a period of a couple of years when I had no friends. During that time, I found my solace in video games—mostly my new GameCube that I received for Christmas in 2001. I also started writing fanfiction about my favorite games (and posting it to a website called Fanfiction.net, which has since been eclipsed by the much-better-from-an-archival-standpoint AO3), and I ended up making some internet friends through this that I'm still friends with today. The internet is truly a gold mine for autistic folks looking to make friends based on shared interests, after all.

The most important takeaway here is that gaming brought me friends. I met my current real-life friend group in high school since we were all in the school Anime Club together, and a large part of our friendship revolved around playing video games together. It's fair to say that playing video games with my friends is still a huge part of maintaining those friendships—when we can't get together to play, we often play together online; and almost every night after work, if you were to look into my apartment for some reason, you'd see my roommate and I playing something or other to de-stress.

The Autistic Gaming Initiative wasn't meant to be a community at first—the plan was to get a team of autistic gamers together and do a relay stream for autistic-run charities (i.e., the Autistic Self Advocacy Network and the Autistic Women and Nonbinary Network). The Autistic Gaming Initiative team still streams on the last weekend of every month—you can usually catch me on Sunday evenings—but the community has become the main focus. We give autistic gamers a space to safely be themselves online without judgment, and we help with social skills, finding friends with mutual interests and hobbies, and even financial aid for each other when applicable.

This is absolutely something you can achieve in your library, on that note! At the library I currently work at (Hoboken Public Library, on the Last Seacoast of Bohemia—er, in Hoboken, New Jersey), a number of teenagers come and hang out in the library after school together every day and play video games and do homework. This is more of an open-ended hangout for them, but providing a safe space for them to engage in their passions and make friends is incredibly important for them, and they definitely respond to it, since we see them every weekday that they have school.

This can be achieved in numerous ways—you can leave it open-ended, like we do, or you can form an actual gaming club at your library. Although ours is basically open gaming time, we hold tournaments from time to time (mostly *Smash Bros.* and *Mario Kart*, because if we did *Splatoon* I would actually enter and obliterate all the kids). Gaming tournaments are a good way to bring in a crowd, and then you can keep them by introducing a gaming club if you so choose. If you're especially interested in working on social skills and cooperation, put the focus on multiplayer co-op games, including traditional board games or tabletop games (Dungeons & Dragons and its ilk have resurged in popularity recently)—it's all gaming!

If you want to especially benefit autistic teenagers who enjoy gaming, here's a few tips:

- Keep it regular.
- Encourage social skills practice!
- Explain to concerned parents and caregivers that gaming provides important social benefits for autistic people.
- Don't put too much pressure on anyone to participate.
- If you're interested in the Autistic Gaming Initiative:
- Website: http://autisticgaming.com/
- Twitter: https://twitter.com/autisticgamers/
- Discord (permanent invite link): https://discordapp.com/invite/9bR2tJX

Hope to see you on Twitch sometime! Just hope you don't run into me in a Ranked Battle in *Splatoon*.

Life Skills

Life skills programming is increasingly popular in libraries for all teens and young adults, not just those who are neurodivergent. ALA lists "emerging adulthood" as a top trend,[3] and library programs on such topics as changing a tire, sewing on a button, and managing finances have become popular. The Slover Library in Norfolk, Virginia, has hosted an inclusive "Adulting 101" series that features sessions on business, career, and financial skills, along with sessions focused on daily living skills such as cooking and using tools to fix things. Lynn Clements, the library's executive director, says that these are some of their most popular programs with both teens and adults. Do a quick Google search for "life skills" or "adulting" programs held at public libraries and you will probably get many results and ideas of what other libraries are successfully implementing with their teens and young adults. Think about which of these programs would work well for your teens, and how you could implement them most successfully.

Many of the examples of low-cost "life skills" programs suggested in this chapter are based on the book *The How-to Handbook* by Martin Oliver and Alexandra Johnson (2014). Karen Jensen of the *Teen Librarian Toolbox* blog suggests setting up a series of programs based on the book's tips and grouped by monthly theme. For example, one theme could be "everyday essentials" and include programs based on the tips "Manage your Money," "Pack a Suitcase," and "Wrap a Gift." All three of these ideas lend themselves well to associated crafts or activities. For example, we described a duct tape wallet craft earlier in the chapter; you might want to tie this in with the "Manage your Money" program. You can search "life hacks" at www.teen librariantoolbox.com for even more ideas.

 MAKE IT VIRTUAL Many life skills activities lend themselves well to the online environment, such as money management. You can also demonstrate topics such as "pack a suitcase" or "wrap a gift" by using your webcam to demonstrate. Have participants log in for a live session so you can discuss in real time, and record the sessions for teens who want to view the program later.

Fandom

While the content of fandoms may change from year to year, it is likely that the teens using your library are fans of something: a TV show, movie, book, celebrity, or game. For autistic teens, you might find that these interests are amplified. Find out what your teens are passionate about and plan programs based on those interests. Maybe it's *Harry Potter*, *Star Wars*, or anime and manga. We can't predict what will be trending as you read this book, and as an adult you may not be able to ascertain on your own what is hot in teen culture, so be sure to check in with your teens before planning. No matter what the topic is, there are easy programs you can plan that will get teens excited. For example, try a cupcake-decorating competition. This is not only a creative activity, but also a competition and a way to make a delicious snack. Provide all of the materials teens need to decorate un-iced cupcakes based on the fandom theme. Teens can then judge who has decorated the best cupcake in various categories—and then they get to eat them! Search "fandom" on Teen Services Underground (www.teen servicesunderground.com) for expanded information about this and other fandom program ideas. You can also plan trivia programs based on the fandom, or create crafts.

MAKE IT VIRTUAL If you're looking for a program that teens can access from home or on their own time, consider introducing a digital escape room. The librarian Sydney Krawiec used Google Forms to create a *Harry Potter*-themed digital escape room that became wildly popular not just with her teens, but also with other librarians interested in replicating the idea.* She has since created a brief YouTube video with instructions for other librarians who want to create their own escape room.**

Post your escape room to your library's Facebook page or YouTube channel so teens can explore it on their own time. Or you can develop a synchronous program by having teens all log in to Zoom at the same time to navigate the room together. This is a great way to encourage team-building and critical thinking—and it can tie in to a "fandom" theme as well.

*https://americanlibrariesmagazine.org/blogs/the-scoop/moving-programming-online

**www.youtube.com/watch?v=xLzbPGF4TzY&t=141s

Photography

Photography is a great hobby for autistic teens. It is essentially a solitary activity, but sharing photos can have a social component. Looking through the viewfinder of a camera is comfortable for someone with central coherence challenges who likes to focus on a detail rather than a whole. Photography can also make it easier for an autistic teen to explore new places and situations. It can even be the centerpiece of an exercise routine. You can use photography as an avenue for multiple program options.

MAKE IT VIRTUAL A photo scavenger hunt works well online. Have teens meet at the beginning and end of the program in an online meeting room. Teens can explore the rooms they are each in, and share pictures with each other by uploading or simply using their webcams to share their phone's digital display. Keep the categories broad to ensure that all teens can participate; for example, "take a picture of something round" or "take a picture of something from a kitchen."

PHOTOGRAPHY SCAVENGER HUNT

Developed by Barbara Klipper

What You'll Need
- Cameras, through smartphones or otherwise
- A printed list of items to find and photograph
- A timer

SAMPLE PROGRAM PLAN

1. First, make a list of items for teens to photograph in the library. Keep the list limited to five items, and do not include people on this list. The list can include items such as "take a picture of a graphic novel cover that has the color blue," or "take a picture of a sign in the library that includes the word 'way.'"

2. Tell teens the boundaries for their search, for example, "all pictures must be taken on the first floor." Set the timer for twenty minutes and send them off, telling them what time to return.

3. Have teens return to your meeting spot or program room, and compare their pictures for each category.

OUTDOOR PHOTOGRAPHY

Developed by Barbara Klipper

What You'll Need
- Cameras, through smartphones or otherwise
- A timer

SAMPLE PROGRAM PLAN

1. If your library has a garden or courtyard, take the teens outside and let them spend a period of time taking photos of objects and scenes, not people.

2. Come back inside and, if you have the capability of uploading the photos and projecting them on a large screen, show what people photographed.

3. Discuss in simple language what they chose, and for the more cognitively able, why they photographed what they did. Others can share what they like about the pictures. Keep it simple and positive. Give concrete suggestions for how to frame comments. For example, "tell us two things you like about ___'s photograph."

Social Networking and Digital Citizenship

Social networking apps and sites give teens a fun way to communicate and stay connected. However, navigating social networking apps and sites can leave teens vulnerable, as they may not understand how to best keep themselves and their information safe. Programs can be designed that both introduce teens to social networking sites and provide tips for keeping them safe online.

Autistic teens in particular might benefit from these programs. Communication and social interaction online can open up a world of engagement they might not find locally. The many groups on these sites create the possibility for an autistic teen to find a community of people who share his special interests. For a teen who has not found a friend group to socialize with locally, the ability to relate to others via social networking can make a huge difference.

Also, for some autistic teens, communication can be easier online than face-to-face. With online social networking, communication doesn't rely on reading body language or facial expressions. With many online platforms, the teen can be in control of the speed of a conversation. This gives a teen time to consider their replies, or even consult with a friend or trusted adult before responding to a post. However, there are still some tricky situations online, and autistic teens in particular might benefit from digital citizenship guidance. For example, autistic teens may not pick up on innuendo or sarcasm in posts, or they may not recognize the clues others send when they don't want to continue a relationship, and may inadvertently harass people online.

Teens will be attracted to programs about social networking apps and sites, but perhaps not to a program about digital citizenship. Because of this, we don't recommend offering a stand-alone digital citizenship program. Instead, you can sprinkle these lessons throughout your more appealing social networking programs. You can use resources such as CommonSense Media (www.commonsensemedia .org) and the book *The Secret Rules of Social Networking* (2015) by Barbara Klipper and Rhonda Shapiro-Rieser for guidance. Infiniteach, a company that creates digital apps to support autistic users, has good free resources for teaching Twitter and YouTube use, along with general internet safety, available on its website.[4] You can provide snippets of digital citizenship guidance while helping teens navigate the latest social media apps and websites. For example, if you are sharing the site Reddit, help your teens explore how to sign up for "subreddits" while introducing the codes of conduct. Tell them that each subreddit has its own code of conduct, show them where to find them on the site, and help them to understand how to apply the code to their own behavior.

We highly recommend that you make your social networking programming for teens inclusive, so that while you might provide guidance, the teens can communicate with and learn from one another.

> **MAKE IT VIRTUAL**
> Digital citizenship education can take place while teens are already online. You can invite teens to meet you in an online room, and share your screen while you explore websites together. This type of programming could work well with peer mentor pairs by inviting each pair to attend the session virtually.

Career Exploration

Autistic adults are woefully unemployed or underemployed when compared to both their neurotypical peers and adults in other disability categories.[5] While it is commonly stated that the STEM fields are a particularly good fit for autistic adults, it is also true that every person is different, and you are likely to find autistic people working in every field. Try hosting an inclusive program series that brings in people from a variety of jobs to talk about their work. Some occupations to try are computer coders, restaurant employees, and entrepreneurs, all of whom can discuss their career paths and current positions. Make sure to invite a diverse lineup of guest speakers, including those who are autistic or neurodivergent, so that all of your teen attendees can relate and so the autistic teens can see that a meaningful life of competitive employment is possible for them. To optimize accessibility, brief your presenters in advance about the communication strategies that work best with autistic teens.

> **MAKE IT VIRTUAL**
> Invite your speakers to join you online through a virtual career program series. By doing this virtually, you can expand both the network of guest speakers and the pool of teen participants. Location is no longer a concern for those who might otherwise be a long drive away.

Library Employment and Leadership Roles

We know that librarianship can be a rewarding career for autistic adults—there are many autistic librarians and library staff members who have shared stories of their careers, including some within the pages of this book. As librarian Charlie Remy says, "My decision to become a librarian wasn't directly related to my autism diagnosis, but I will say that libraries can be good places for autistic people to work."[6] Use this knowledge as an opportunity to help teens who show an interest in your library to build their career readiness and on-the-job skills. While it is possible these teens will view librarianship as a career and go on to find employment in libraries, they may also choose to follow a different direction. Either way, offering teens meaningful on-the-job training and the chance to practice serving in leadership roles will help them emerge as more confident, independent, and workforce-ready young adults.

Teen Volunteers

It's likely that your library already uses volunteers, including teenage volunteers. Perhaps teens are volunteering to earn credit hours for scholarships or school leadership groups, or to fulfill school requirements for community service. Or they may simply be looking to get involved in their communities, or have an activity they enjoy after school. It's possible that you are already working with autistic teen volunteers and you just don't know it—or maybe you have a hunch but have not had that conversation. Whether you are working with teens that you suspect might be autistic, or you are deliberately recruiting or working with those who you know have a diagnosis, this section will address things to do that will help you to better empathize with, understand, and support your autistic teen volunteers.

Inclusive Hiring Practices

Before teens get a volunteer position, they typically have to go through an interview or application process. You should review and revise your hiring practices to ensure they are inclusive and fair for your autistic teens. As librarian Kate Thompson says: "We often discriminate unintentionally with hiring practices, and I'm interested in the ways we can widen the net. For example, the public library where I currently work had several short essay questions as the first round of interviews, rather than a phone call. This gives people with social anxiety another way to express their ideas in a less time-pressured way." Be mindful of the things you've learned about autism, and don't expect autistic potential volunteers to make eye contact with you or to be tactful in their responses to questions. These behaviors have no bearing on their ability to be valued volunteers for your library.

Positions and Skills

It's not possible to say that there is any one library volunteer position that autistic teens prefer over any other. Autistic teens, just like anybody else, have individual interests, skills, and abilities, and there are many ways that they can both learn from and support the library through a mutually beneficial relationship. While some teens will decide to build on these experiences through a future career in libraries or information organization, what's important to remember is that these teens are learning how to navigate the workplace in general. Try to think beyond what your library needs and instead provide meaningful, transferable, on-the-job opportunities.

Some teens will feel more comfortable interacting with the public, working independently, or having a variety of tasks to perform. It all depends on the individual. Have a conversation with each teen to determine how you can embark on a mutually beneficial partnership. Tech-savvy teens can use their volunteer hours to design a schedule for your other teen volunteers or help you set up spreadsheets and enter data, making the record-keeping part of your summer reading club much easier. They can check for dead links on your library's website. They can even do behind-the-scenes tasks like counting out and bundling reading club incentives.

Teens who need more support can volunteer for short periods of time doing repetitive and predictable tasks like cleaning books and toys used in children's programs, or cutting shapes with Ellison dies. The Ferguson Library has used these shapes as part of its children's summer reading club for years, and thousands are needed over the course of the program. Remember that while it might require extra work on the part of the librarian to set up and supervise these tasks, the goal is not quantity or speed of production. Instead, you should view the exercise not only as a way to get the jobs done, but also as a means of integrating these teens into the community and giving them a sense of purpose and achievement.

All teens will benefit from learning and practicing both technical skills and what are known as soft skills, such as the following ones:

- Time management
- Communicating with coworkers
- Reporting to a supervisor
- Working on a team
- Problem-solving
- Dressing appropriately for work

Consider focusing on these skills as you train and work with teen volunteers.

LIBRARIANSHIP AND AUTISM
Tina Dolcetti

2012 was a year of new beginnings. A new career as a children's librarian at Moose Jaw Public Library. A new city and province, and a new diagnosis of autism spectrum disorder. While the assessment revealed some difficulties, it highlighted many of the benefits of having an autism spectrum disorder, particularly in the area of librarianship.

What brings sparkle to your days and a spring to your step? Is it hearing your favorite music, or learning something new about an exciting topic? For a librarian with an autism spectrum disorder (or an autistic librarian), a special interest can be an asset to the library when it is linked to library goals.

What do *My Little Pony*, *Minecraft*, and *Doctor Who* all have in common? All have dedicated novels, information books, graphic novels, media channels and fandoms for popular programming. A special interest in any one of these topics by a caring librarian with autism can ensure a complete collection, or turn non-reader fans into lifelong readers.

A special interest by a young adult volunteer with autism can be a gold mine for the hiring library. When I was creating a *Minecraft* program for the library, I knew that I did not have the enthusiasm for *Minecraft* that our autistic youth embodied, and that was important to the success of the program. I obtained permission to hire her with an honorarium to assist me in leading the programs.

It was a win-win situation. Her innate skills and sophisticated *Minecraft* knowledge gave our program credibility. Our students developed a rapport and admiration for our young leader. Our young leader later transitioned into a student work placement at the library, which was critical to her continued attendance at her high school.

Offering More Support

If you have an autistic teen volunteer who needs additional support, think about implementing the following to help ensure a positive experience for all:

- Speak to the teen (or parent if necessary) beforehand to address the following:
    Do you (or your teen) have special interests? If so, what are they?
    Do you (or your teen) have sensory sensitivities? If so, what will make you more comfortable?
    Do you (or your teen) work alone, or will you work better with more supervision and/or guidance? Is there a type of guidance that is most helpful? For example, will visual supports or a written sequence of the steps involved in the task help you understand what needs to be done?

Will you (or your teen) prefer doing the same thing each time you come, or will you want some variety?

Is attention span an issue? What is the ideal amount of time for you (or your teen) to volunteer each time?

- The first time the volunteer comes, have two or three tasks in mind that they can do. Ask which of these they prefer. Show them the job they select in several ways: in writing, by modeling what to do, and verbally. Teach the job one step at a time. It may be helpful to prepare a checklist of the steps in the project that the teen can follow. If they don't have a preference, pick one to start with. If they don't like the task after trying it out, move on to one of your other possibilities.
- Build routine and predictability into the volunteer job. Have the volunteer come at the same day and time each week, and have some of the same tasks for them to perform. If possible, have them work with the same staff person each time they come. If their regular supervisor will not be available, find out if they are comfortable working with someone else or if they would prefer to skip that work session.
- Build in breaks between more sedentary activities for stretching, walking, or otherwise moving around.
- Help with transitions by giving ten- and five-minute warnings as the volunteer time is coming to an end.
- Find out if fidgets or a stim are helpful, and allow their use during volunteer sessions. For jobs that involve the public, identify a place the volunteer can go to if they need to stim.

Working with Autism-Specific Groups

In addition to working with teens individually as volunteers, you can consider bringing teens in as a group. Most high school classes for autistic teens teach them pre-vocational skills as part of their curriculum. You may be able to partner with a teacher in this effort and have a class come to the library for an hour or two each week to volunteer. If you decide to do this, keep the following points in mind:

- Meet first with the teacher to discuss what the class is capable of, what sensory issues you might encounter, and what tasks the group might enjoy.
- Identify a couple of jobs that they can realistically accomplish for the library that will also be a learning opportunity for them.
- Once the jobs are identified, ask the teacher to assist in breaking them down into small tasks, and to design a visual schedule or checklist that describes the steps of the activity.
- If possible, schedule the volunteer visits for the same time each week.
- Provide a relatively quiet and distraction-free area for the teens to work.

- Make sure that the teacher will be available to act as a job coach.
- Be sure to acknowledge the work these teens have done each time they come, and at the end of the semester or school year.

For all volunteers, always remember that the outcome is not just about what the teen can do for the library, but also how your library can help these teens. Work with your volunteers to ensure they feel empowered as members of the library team. Check in often to make sure your approach is working, and find ways that teens can grow in their responsibilities when they feel ready.

Teen Advisory Board Participation

Participating on a teen library advisory board is another way that teens can volunteer and gain leadership and decision-making experience. These groups tend to be inclusive and welcoming, and are often a great opportunity for teens to socialize and make friends. If you have a teen advisory board, it's quite possible that you already have autistic teens in your group. You can also be proactive and recruit individual teens that you know, if you feel this could be a meaningful opportunity for them. Sometimes this is as simple as approaching a regular patron with a personal invitation to come to a meeting. Or you can reach out to autism groups in your community to identify teens who are searching for ways to become involved with other teens and in the community. Make sure your advisory board uses inclusive practices so that all members, including those who are autistic, feel welcomed and feel like part of the team. At the Ferguson Library, Barbara's teen group had autistic members, and the group helped select music for the teen collection, pick the theme for the teen summer reading club, and decorate the children's room for the winter holidays, among other things. Participation can be one way that autistic teens can get to develop and practice leadership skills.

 **MAKE IT VIRTUAL** Advisory board meetings can be held just as easily online as they can in person. Even if you have a meeting at your library, make sure there is an option for participants to join online as well.

Autism-Specific Program Ideas to Try

Though inclusive programs are best for most, some groups of autistic teens will need more focused support when they attend library programs, and will prefer autism-specific programs. Groups that provide social support for autistic teens can be found in many communities, and some of these groups meet in their local public libraries. Many schools with self-contained autism programs enjoy bringing students to the library for regular field trips. If you are lucky enough to be a host site for these groups already, you have a ready audience for your programming. Try moving beyond simply offering space for them in your meeting rooms, and instead provide interactive sessions that might appeal to their interests. Ask the group leaders and the teens what they would value most from a library-led program, and you can even ask for guidance about what types of supports will be the most helpful.

If you don't have groups already meeting at your library, there are multiple ways to still engage with autistic teens in your community who might benefit from autism-specific programming. You might do a search online through sites like Meetup.com to see if there are already autism groups in your community. If you find some, invite them to consider moving their meeting location to the free spaces offered at the library, or go to them where they already meet. Doing this type of outreach is a great way to start building relationships with these community members. Renee Grassi describes outreach as one of the best ways to make connections in the community, and she provides drop-in library programming at community events for families with disabilities.

Peer Mentor Programs

For autistic teens who are interested in connecting and fitting in with their peers but who need a little more support, a peer mentoring program series could be a great fit. Peer mentoring programs are typically longer-term arrangements rather than one-shot programs. After all, relationships take time to build. Try a timeline arranged around the school year, taking these partnerships one semester or a quarter at a time. Since these relationships work best when the pairs meet on a regular basis, try to have a weekly meeting time. To set a buddy program up, you'll need to do the following things:

1. Recruit potential mentors. Try reaching out to your local school's honor societies, since many of these teens need volunteering opportunities. Mentors must be able to meet regularly, and provide guidance and encouragement through all scheduled activities. Mentors should be excited about the opportunity, not just willing or doing it grudgingly because they need the credit. The best partnerships develop when both members are invested in the partnership's success and see each other as equals. The mentor's actual commitment can vary widely based on the programs you plan, so be sure to explain your expectations when you recruit.

2. Provide training and education for mentors. This can be as simple as giving them materials on autism to read, or you can invite an autism expert or self-advocate from your community to provide basic information and train them. Make sure the training includes information about "ableism" (discrimination or prejudice against people who have disabilities) and how to avoid it. At the Skokie Public Library, "Friendship Ambassadors" for its Friend Squad are trained to support peers who see the world differently than they do.

3. Pair the teens up based on shared goals and interests. Consider having pairs agree to a set of shared rules for their mentoring relationship. A good example from higher education can be found at the National Mentoring Resource Center.[7]

4. Arrange for regular weekly meetings at the library. Ideally, all partner dyads will meet at the same time, though you may need to allow some flexibility based on the teens' schedules. We recommend setting up meeting spaces in your teen room or other library common area so the pairs are not segregated from the rest of the library. Be sure to provide snacks as an incentive. Greet teens at the beginning, and say goodbye at the end, but otherwise allow them to build relationships largely without adult intervention.

5. Plan for a concluding event. Throughout the weekly sessions, have the pairs work toward a final event. This could be an art show, a dance, a cooking demonstration, a gaming event, or really anything else that interests your teens. Planning for an event in weekly meetings will provide structure, and the event itself will be a fun reward.

6. Check in frequently and individually with each mentor and mentee to ensure the relationship is moving forward in a positive direction and goals are being met. Let pairs have space when meeting to just hang out and be teens, but let them know where you are and that you are available at any time during their meetings. Mentoring programs depend on personal dynamics, and there is the potential for conflict in some partnerships. Even if both teens are in the relationship for the right reasons, it is still possible that their individual personalities might not align well. If you check in with both participants regularly, you'll catch problems quickly and be able to reorganize or rethink the program's structure if needed.

Peer mentoring can take on various forms, but the important thing is that relationships are developed. You may use the weekly meeting times to focus on a particular set of skills, such as social networking, digital literacy, or life skills, or you may focus just on planning an event. Many of the programs we describe in this chapter would work well in a peer mentoring situation, from gaming to gardening. Take the time to assess what will work best for members of your community, and plan your mentoring goals accordingly.

Programs to Promote Career Readiness

We already talked about the importance of offering autistic teens the chance to learn and practice career preparation skills through volunteering and inclusive programming; it is equally important to provide opportunities for teens who need more support to develop these skills. Librarian Ryan Moniz did this and won the Young Adult Library Services Association's Innovation Award in 2019 for the work he did with the "Essential Skills" program at the Markham Public

Library in Ontario, Canada. After learning of the need for programs and services for teens aging out of supports, Moniz reached out to the local community group Community Living York South, and a partnership was formed. Together, they developed a curriculum to teach digital literacy skills to these teens in a supportive social environment.

Moniz says that knowing your own community's needs is important: "The piece I always try and encourage people to start with is: look at your community and understand who's there [to partner with] us as librarians. We often think that if we're not the expert in something, we don't really want to touch it, and that's fine. You don't have to be the expert. What's important is using your research skills, and finding out who is out there [to partner with]."

In the "Essential Skills" program series, teens learned technical skills that are important for navigating our digital world, starting with basic mouse and keyboarding skills and building up to internet safety and cyberbullying. Moniz built life skills lessons into the curriculum as well. For example, the group discussed bus schedules and played out scenarios about getting to important meetings on time. These lessons were immediately applied to their lives—in the final sessions the teens, along with their aides, began taking the bus to the library for programs. Moniz suggests incorporating a short game to play at the beginning and end of each session. He used a simple computer game in which you click on frogs to "feed them" flies as they jump back and forth between lily pads. This not only helps to build fine motor skills, but it also adds both consistency and a fun element to every session program.

MAKE IT VIRTUAL

Host an online group to practice technical skills. As one session's lesson plan, try introducing participants to the mouse and keyboarding lessons provided by CommonSense Media.* Invite teens to join at the same time, introduce the lesson, and ask them all to participate in their own virtual environments, and then ask them to meet back in the online room thirty minutes later to wrap up.

*www.commonsense.org/education/lesson-plans/lessons-for-little-learners-mouse-skills.

Arts and Crafts

With the help of an "Autism Welcome Here" grant and a great team effort, teen librarian Dianne Aimone, working closely with two parents of autistic teens, Lisa Currao and Kerry Boland, along with staff members Laurie Angle and Jody DeGroat, provided programs for autistic teens at the Albert Wisner Public Library (Orange County, NY). They found the most successful aspects of their series were "when the teens on the spectrum allowed their imaginations to run and create astonishing and frankly unexpected original works of art."[8] During the program, an art teacher brought many tools and materials, the program was well-organized, and multiple adults were available to assist. With a willing art teacher and a variety of art supplies, these programs can be easily replicated.

ART APPRECIATION AND CREATION

Albert Wisner Public Library, Warwick, New York
Developed by Dianne Aimone, Kerry Boland, Laurie Angle, Jody Degroat,
and Lisa Currao (with modifications by Barbara Klipper and Amelia Anderson)

Time Needed: One hour

What You'll Need
- Washable paint, brushes, and paper. Make sure to have some adaptive supplies like easy-to-grip brushes.
- Other art supplies such as found objects, items with texture like sandpaper and soft fabric, glue, stickers, paper with patterns or designs, scissors, stickers, washi tape, and so on.
- Tarp or newsprint to protect tables
- Projector
- A visual schedule

SAMPLE PROGRAM PLAN

1. Welcome participants and review the program's schedule, which is posted on the wall, written on a dry erase board, or printed on a sheet given to each participant.

2. Introduce the art teacher, who will then share a PowerPoint presentation of ten well-known works of art. For each piece, the teacher should introduce the title of the piece and the artist's name, talk briefly about one aspect of the painting and its relation to emotions, and engage the participants in a discussion, asking open-ended questions about how they feel about the painting and why. Repeat this sequence for each work of art. You might find that your participants will be ready to move on to creating their own artwork before you discuss all ten works; shorten this discussion as you see fit.

3. After the discussion, give the teens instruction and support to create their own artwork based on the famous works they've just seen and discussed, using the materials provided (pencils, glue, fabric, found objects of different textures, paint, etc.).

SIP AND PAINT

Albert Wisner Public Library, Warwick, New York
Developed by Dianne Aimone, Kerry Boland, Laurie Angle, Jody Degroat,
and Lisa Currao (adapted by Barbara Klipper and Amelia Anderson)

Time Needed: One hour

What You'll Need

- Paint, brushes (including easy-grip ones), and paper
- An assortment of other art supplies—glue, scissors, found objects, items with texture like cotton balls, sandpaper and soft fabric, stickers, colored and patterned papers
- Tarp or newsprint to protect tables
- Projector
- Snacks
- A visual schedule

SAMPLE PROGRAM PLAN

Before the Program

The art teacher or librarian draws an outline of a famous work of art for each participant, either on tracing paper or by projecting and copying the image. Well-known simple works like *Sunflowers* by Vincent Van Gogh are good choices for this program. The original work is projected on a screen or is available as a print reproduction for each program participant.

At the Program

1. Welcome the participants and review the program's schedule.
2. Explain the proper way to hold a brush and how to make brushstrokes.
3. Project the original work of art on a screen or hand out copies of a printed reproduction to each program participant.
4. Explain and show how to fill in the outline of their picture and copy details from the original image.
5. After copying the famous painting, tell the teens they can use the materials provided to create their own original artworks.
6. Throughout the program, allow the teens to take breaks to chat with others, stim or pace if needed, and enjoy snacks.

Dance

Librarians at the Albert Wisner Public Library found that the most successful programs they offered for their autistic teens provided hands-on opportunities, movement, and outlets for creative expression. Along with art, dance programming meets these requirements, and dance programs proved to be quite a hit at that library. Dance is a creative outlet, and it allows an opportunity for interacting with peers. It also provides much-needed physical movement after a long day of sitting in school.

The following two programs, successfully implemented at the Albert Wisner Public Library, are especially well-suited for a peer mentoring program. It only makes sense that teens would want to learn the latest moves from their peers, not adults! The first program supports creativity and movement, while the second is more focused on learning the skills needed for dancing socially.

MODERN DANCE AND MOVEMENT

Albert Wisner Public Library, Warwick, New York
Developed by Dianne Aimone, Kerry Boland, Laurie Angle, Jody Degroat,
and Lisa Currao

Time Needed: One hour

What You'll Need
- Music and speakers
- Poster board
- Mirrors for teens to see themselves (optional)
- A program leader—ideally, a dance teacher who is proficient in modern, creative, and/or improvisational dance

SAMPLE PROGRAM PLAN

Before the program, prepare large cards or posters. Each poster should spell out in text and illustrate a different movement instruction, for example, gallop, shake, walk on tiptoe, or ice skate.

At the Program
1. Welcome teens to the program with introductions, a movement game, and some warm-up exercises.
2. Display the movement cards while reading them aloud. Teen mentors or other dance instructors can help at this point by demonstrating each movement as it is presented.
3. Play music, and ask the teens to act out the moves, as well as make up their own.
4. Demonstrate how the teens can make shapes with their bodies (for example, a tree) and support them in trying these moves, then have them "melt" to the floor, letting their whole bodies relax and lie down. Again, mentors or volunteers can help with verbal instructions or by modeling the moves.

5. Invite the teens to leap or jump over an item placed in the middle of the floor.

6. Then guide the teens in a mirror exercise done with a partner, in which they face each other and take turns initiating a movement and trying to copy their partner's movement while it is being done.

This plan incorporates many elements of dance, and is intended to give you an idea of what a program can include. You can add, remove, or modify movements to fit whatever your instructor and the teens are most comfortable with.

SOCIAL DANCING

Albert Wisner Public Library, Warwick, New York
Developed by librarian Dianne Aimone , Kerry Boland, Laurie Angle,
Jody Degroat, and Lisa Currao

Time Needed: One hour

What You'll Need
- Music and speakers
- Mirrors for teens to see themselves (optional)
- Snacks
- A program leader—either a dance teacher or a librarian

SAMPLE PROGRAM PLAN

1. Welcome the teens and begin the program with each participant introducing themselves by name.

2. Share the rules of etiquette for slow dancing, such as how to ask someone to dance, how to accept or decline an invitation to dance, where to properly put one's hands while slow dancing, and how close to stand to your partner. Use a written and/or visual handout to reinforce the verbal explanation.

3. Lead teens through popular dances and dances they might participate in at weddings or school dances (for example, the Electric Slide). Ask teen mentors/buddies to assist.

4. Break for snacks and socializing.

The programs suggested here for art and dance would work well for students on a field trip to the public library, as a series, as stand-alone programs for teens after school, or for teen mentor programs. As always, you should determine what would best support the teens in your community, and tailor these ideas to fit your library's goals.

Final Thoughts

Some teens will already be library users, having grown up attending storytimes and children's programs. Others may be unfamiliar with the library as a fun and supportive community space. Think about ways you can reach out to teen members of your local autism community who are not already library users, to let them know you have inclusive services and programs they might enjoy. Invite them personally to programs you think they will find especially interesting. Introducing autistic teens to library services and programs allows them to socialize, learn, have fun, and plug into their communities. Perhaps even more importantly, these opportunities connect them with the idea of the library as a free community service that is permanently available to them as they navigate life beyond the services provided for them through secondary education.

NOTES

1. Xin Wei, Jennifer W. Yu, Paul Shattuck, Mary McCracken, and Jose Blackorby, "Science, Technology, Engineering, and Mathematics (STEM) Participation among College Students with an Autism Spectrum Disorder." *Journal of Autism and Developmental Disorders* 43, no. 7 (2013): 1539–46.

2. Micah O. Mazurek, Christopher R. Engelhardt, and Kelsey E. Clark, "Video Games from the Perspective of Adults with Autism Spectrum Disorder." *Computers in Human Behavior* 51 (2015): 122–30.

3. Library of the Future, "Emerging Adulthood," American Library Association, www.ala.org/tools/future/trends/emergingadulthood.

4. Infiniteach, "Tweet All About It! Teaching Tweeting and YouTube," https://infiniteach.com/resources/tweet-all-about-it-braingame-using -twitter-youtube/; see also "Internet Safety Plan for Your Child with Autism," https://infiniteach.com/resources/internet-safety-plan-for-your -child-with-autism/.

5. Paul T. Shattuck et al., "Postsecondary Education and Employment among Youth with an Autism Spectrum Disorder," *Pediatrics* 129, no. 6 (2012): 1042–49.

6. Alice Eng, "Neurodiversity in the Library: One Librarian's Experience," In the Library with the Lead Pipe, June 28, 2017, www.inthelibrarywith theleadpipe.org/2017/neurodiversity-in-the-library/.

7. Catriona Mowat, Anna Cooper, and Lee Gilson, "Supporting Students on the Autism Spectrum," National Autistic Society, 2011, https://national mentoringresourcecenter.org/index.php/component/k2/item/340-supporting -students-on-the-autism-spectrum-student-mentor-guidelines.html.

8. Albert Wisner Public Library, "End-of-Year Report," www.librariesand autism.org/grant/AlbertWisnerPL2018Autism_End_Year_Report.pdf.

Programming for Families

ONE MOTHER OF AUTISTIC CHILDREN HAD THIS TO SAY ABOUT HER experience: "Since my [autistic] twins were born, we've pretty much overhauled all of our activities and traditions. We do holidays differently. For instance, instead of watching the parade from the street, we hang out in a hotel room right above it. We go on different outings. Our area has an active autism community with tons of activities. So we stick to the sensory-friendly events where we know there's no pressure. And we only spend time with people who are on board with accommodating [our children's] needs. Because that's what parents are supposed to do—understand what their children need, and plan life accordingly. And you know what? I love our new lifestyle (not that it's always a walk in the park). I love our new (and tried-and-true) friends. And I love to see my children happy."[1]

Many parents who have an autistic child will be able to identify with this parent's comments, while others may be overwhelmed by the changes in their lives. Parents, however, will not be the only ones who have such experiences and reactions. Siblings, grandparents, caregivers, and members of the more extended family may also find that their lives are different from the lives of their peers. They may feel a special bond with others who share these experiences, and they may need support and information as they navigate the situations they encounter.

As a facility that serves everyone in the community, the public library is uniquely able to reach out to all of the people surrounding an autistic child. Librarians already do this to some extent when they chat with parents or other caregivers who bring their children to programs, and when they use program activities to model ways for families to engage with their children at home. However, libraries also have the opportunity to reach out further by offering services and programs that address the specific needs of parents and other family members. These needs often take two forms: the support these family members may need for themselves as they navigate the world and relate to their autistic family member, and their need for education about the ways they can support the autistic child in their family. Additionally, because family members often serve as advocates for their autistic children, the library can help with resources to support them in these efforts, providing everything from guides to the IEP process (i.e., an individualized education program), to information and referral services that point family members to special education attorneys, speech and occupational therapists, and community-based groups where they can learn how to be an ally from other families.

The 2020 ASAN book *Welcome to the Autistic Community* describes the important role families can play: "Families can be strong allies for their autistic family members. Many years ago, parents of disabled kids started getting together. They worked to close institutions, and fought for their kids to get support in the community. Parents are still fighting today for the rights of their kids. You can be a part of that fight, too! Families can make a big difference for their family members. You can support your autistic family member to have a good life, and help fight for our rights. You can make sure your family is a safe place for us, and help other families be allies, too."[2]

While we don't know the exact cause of autism, we do know that there is a genetic component to the disorder. Autism is more common in the siblings of children with a diagnosis than in those without,[3] and many parents receive an autism diagnosis as adults only after their child is diagnosed. Creating more inclusive spaces and services for autistic children may very well support their family members, who may also have a diagnosis or who may be autistic without having a diagnosis yet, or even realizing it.

It's also important to remember that not all families look the same, and autism is intersectional. In an essay in the collection *All the Weight of Our Dreams: On Living Racialized Autism*, Dee Phair writes: "I'm Black. I'm a woman. I'm the child of immigrants. I'm a mother. I'm autistic. And I know there are more people like me somewhere."[4] Think about ways you can provide inclusive, culturally sensitive programs for all of the families your library serves, while bearing in mind that communities made up predominantly of people of color often get overlooked by agencies that provide autism-related services. These are the communities that could benefit the most from the library's services and information.

No matter what your library environment is, it is important to consider the whole family. School librarians may also find opportunities to work with family members through outreach and special events, or perhaps by working with siblings attending the same school as the autistic family member. In this chapter, we present some ideas for ways you can serve the family members of a child on the autism spectrum.

Programs and Services for Parents and Caregivers

Parents and caregivers whose children have an autism diagnosis need both support and information, and you can help meet both of these needs through library programs. Reach out to parents and caregivers as they bring their children to your storytime or teen programming and find out what their needs are and how the library can help. It is always best to be guided by your audience as you plan programming. They may want the library to set up a support group or offer information sessions, but before you do, check with your local school district to make sure that you're not duplicating their efforts.

Informal Parents and Caregivers' Group

You can support parents and caregivers by creating informal opportunities for them to meet and share with each other. All you need to provide is a free meeting space, refreshments, and some publicity. For a drop-in networking and socializing group, you should try making the space available once a month.

Provide Information Sessions

As an alternative, you can create a more formal group for parents, with a trained discussion leader and guest speakers. Reach out to community organizations, particularly those run by autistic self-advocates, for help with publicizing the program and for assistance locating qualified speakers or facilitators. Leave time at the beginning or the end of these more structured sessions for parents to socialize with one another and build their community of support.

Some topics that will be useful to parents include:

- Inclusive summer camps and other recreational opportunities
- Parents' rights under the IDEA (Individuals with Disabilities Education Act)
- Early intervention—how to access services for children from birth to age three
- A speaker from your local Parent Training and Information Center (www .parentcenterhub.org)
- A panel of parents with older children who can talk about what to expect as the children grow
- How to choose the best autism apps
- Dealing with your own feelings and expectations for your child

You can also offer speakers or workshops on these topics and others as one-time events that are open to the entire community.

TANDEM YOUTH AND
CAREGIVER PROGRAMS

Kate Thompson

Through the ALSC Mentorship Program I was assigned a wonderful mentor, Maria Papanastassiou. She has been working on adaptive programs at her library, the Arlington Heights (IL) Memorial Library, for several years. Together we developed an idea I had that came out of my own experiences as a parent using the library. Since it can be hard to attend programs due to a lack of trained care providers, we created a tandem event where youth are doing one program and caregivers are doing another in the same room. This enables parents to feel comfortable that their children are within eyesight, but also gives them the opportunity to network with their fellow parents and learn something new. Other caregivers are often our best resources.

For example, we did an individualized education program (IEP) binder event for caregivers and provided them with materials and ideas so they could spend some time organizing that all-important paperwork. Meanwhile, the youth had a LEGO party with the other staffer. We asked a local parent advocate to attend the program to assist with any basic questions, and we made certain to include information about other local resources.

Librarian Holly Jin of the Skokie Public Library also found success with a tandem program, Skokie's "Club Wonder," which was offered monthly during the school year for children (ages 3 to 8) and their parents or caregivers. Jin conducted a sensory storytime for the children, while guest presenters from the community provided informational programming for the parents and caregivers. Among the guest presenters were a musician, a physical therapist who specialized in yoga, an occupational therapist who discussed picky eating, and a recreational therapist who talked about the importance of sensory play. Registration was requested, so attendance could be limited to twenty people and so staff and presenters could find out in advance a little about each child in attendance. As Jin describes it, the program was an opportunity for learning—librarians and professionals were able to share and learn from each other about the services that each provides, and parents and caregivers were able to connect with and learn from each other in small groups.

MAKE IT VIRTUAL

Parent and caregiver sessions can be provided online. You can record live sessions and make them available for streaming later, or host a live Zoom session in which parents and caregivers can still connect and socialize after the session is over.

Programs and Services for Siblings

The siblings of autistic children can also benefit from library programming. Despite parents' best intentions, siblings may not receive appropriate attention and may be left with conflicting feelings of love, worry, jealousy, embarrassment, guilt, and anger. Although such emotions are common in many sibling relationships, when a child's sibling is diagnosed with autism or another disability, their feelings may be more pronounced and complex.

In her article "Considering the Needs of Siblings of Individuals with Asperger Profiles," Carol M. Singer identifies four broad areas in which the siblings of autistic children need support:

1. Siblings need developmentally appropriate information about autism.
2. Children need the opportunity to express their feelings about their autistic siblings, and to have those feelings validated.
3. Siblings need to have their parents' expectations of them clarified. They especially may need help understanding why their parents may have different rules for them than they do for their autistic siblings. They might also need help understanding why their parents may require their assistance or support in working with the autistic family member.
4. Siblings need help building their own community of support and understanding how to respond to peer and community reactions to their family. One place they can get this help and support is in a safe group of their peers who also have autistic or neurodivergent siblings.[5]

When designing programming for siblings, and when including them in programming with their family members, make sure to address as many of these concerns as you can in your program design.

Welcoming Siblings within Inclusive Programming

If you offer inclusive programming, siblings will already be able to participate, but make sure they feel welcome in these programs. One way to ensure this is to be careful to pay attention to all participants, not just those who need extra help or direction. Siblings may already feel overlooked or ignored if their brother or sister typically receives more attention than they do. Don't exacerbate these feelings in your programs. Instead, be careful to provide equal opportunities in your inclusive programming for every child and to praise neurotypical attendees as often as you praise autistic ones.

Welcoming Siblings in Autism-Specific Programming

Children may not always enjoy tagging along to programs designed for their autistic siblings. However, sometimes it works best for families' schedules to bring everyone to the library at the same time, and older siblings might find themselves in a sensory storytime whether they like it or not. The siblings may well end up enjoying these programs too, but it is also possible that, depending on their age, they may feel left out or forced to sit through a "baby" program. One way to address this is to provide a space with toys or craft materials that siblings can use while their parents and the autistic child are attending the program. Bring in a teen volunteer or two to supervise and keep track of the materials. Any type of passive programming can work well in these circumstances—just provide the materials and supplies, and let children use their imaginations. *Sesame Street* has a printable packet, "The Sibling Experience" that encourages autism siblings to explore their feelings through creative journaling.[6] You can print out copies of the packet and have them available for siblings to work through during the program. Or, if a number of siblings are regular tag-alongs, you can provide something not related to autism at all, like a giant puzzle the siblings can work on together, or a board game they can play with each other. Working together on projects or games will facilitate the siblings' interaction with one another and may lead to friendships or the development of support networks. Just be sure the teen volunteer is comfortable controlling the noise level if the siblings get too engrossed and loud as they play.

You can also consider enlisting older sibs to serve as helpers in your targeted or inclusive storytime programs. They can serve as the teen volunteers who supervise the younger siblings in attendance, or they can assist you by distributing and collecting materials for program activities or creating visual supports for the program. Some siblings may feel important and enjoy doing this while others may resist, finding it too close to the role they play at home. Make the offer and let the children decide if and how they want to be part of the program.

Stand-Alone Sibling Programs

Siblings may benefit from programs designed just for them, especially when they have the chance to connect with other children who have similar family experiences. Think about some of the following examples for how you can provide opportunities for siblings to learn, explore, and connect.

Sibshops

Sibshops are organized workshops for the siblings of children with disabilities, run by trained leaders. The Sibshop curriculum offers a combination of fun activities and a chance for these children to interact with their peers. To find out if there is a Sibshop program in your area that you can bring into the library, visit their website (www .siblingsupport.org/sibshops). Or, if you are

MAKE IT VIRTUAL
If there are no active Sibshops groups locally, you can connect your siblings through their virtual communities, which you can search by age and even location.

really passionate about their mission and want to bring a Sibshop group to your community, you can become a facilitator yourself through a paid online training process.

Book Discussions

Another thing you can do for siblings is to organize a book club just for them. Keep the meetings short (less than one hour) and incorporate crafts. Tune in to what the siblings say they need. While some may seem to have "autism fatigue," it is likely that most of them will be interested in learning more about autism and talking about the family and sibling commonalities among their peers. For middle-grade siblings, you can do a book discussion using a fiction book they can relate to. For younger children, try a picture book about an autistic sibling pair, like *My Brother Charlie* by Holly Robinson Peete and Ryan Elizabeth Peete, illustrated by Shane Evans. If your group isn't interested in reading about autism, try offering titles that deal more broadly with siblings and family dynamics. One notable example is *The Penderwicks: A Summer Tale of Four Sisters, Two Rabbits, and a Very Interesting Boy*, by Jeanne Birdsall, and the other books in that series.

MAKE IT VIRTUAL Move your book discussions online and have live meetings with siblings through web conferencing software such as Zoom.

Autism Acceptance Programs

You can find out if older siblings are interested in helping you plan an "autism acceptance event" for the community. Many libraries host events of this kind in April, which is Autism Acceptance Month. Siblings often have lots of good ideas, and may have an interest in sharing this part of their lives with others. Here are some other programs to consider developing:

Art exhibits: Siblings may enjoy creating works of art that depict their families and reveal their feelings about their siblings. Or they can create posters that teach about autism. You can display these in the library or post them online in a virtual gallery.

Videos: Siblings may also enjoy helping you prepare a video of your storytime or other programs that can be posted on the library's website or shown at a community program.

In general, though, you should consider offering programming about autism at other times of the year, not just April. Relegating a topic or community group to its designated month is "othering" and adds to the perception that these people need special treatment and can be ignored the rest of the year. As part of a culture of inclusion, try to offer disability acceptance programming throughout the year.

MAKE IT VIRTUAL Art exhibits can be displayed online in a virtual gallery, and videos can be posted online through the library's website or social media channels.

Offer Programs Unrelated to Autism

Finally, siblings need special time in which they are not focused on being a brother or sister to a neurodivergent child. Even children who love their siblings need to be recognized and supported as individuals. At these programs you can show a movie, make crafts, or play video games. It is important for siblings to have the chance to just be kids, to be silly and have fun in whatever programming you already provide for their peers. Make sure to offer them opportunities to do this.

Programs and Services for Grandparents

The non-custodial grandparents of autistic children are frequently overlooked, but they often play a major role in the family, and they also have needs that the library can help meet. Evidence of the key role that grandparents play can be found in the results of a 2017 survey of the grandparents of autistic children and teens; grandparents reported experiencing challenges as well as great positivity in their roles.[7]

Host Support Groups

Grandparents are interested in learning more about autism, and many of them want to participate in advocacy efforts. They can be included in the informational programs you provide for parents, but they also appreciate their own private forum for expressing their feelings and for discussing their concerns about such things as the well-being of their adult children, whether or not to give advice, and how to deal with adult children who seem to be in denial about the grandchildren's autistic characteristics. You can provide this by hosting formal or informal support groups for grandparents, similar to the ones you provide for parents. There are resources you can tap into as you design a program. Check out the Grandparent Autism Network (www.ganinfo.org), which operates out of Orange County in California, for a good model and source of information on support for grandparents.

MAKE IT VIRTUAL Grandparent support meetings can easily be held in person or online, based on what your community members prefer. Or you can consider modeling a program on the virtual grandparents' groups hosted by the Asperger/Autism Network (AANE).* In addition to basing your own program on their work, you can provide information about these groups to the grandparents in your community, so they know that a number of options for connection and support are available to them.

*www.aane.org/resources/family-and-friends/support-and-social-groups-grandparents

Host Programs for Grandparents and Their Grandchildren

Libraries can also provide a welcoming space for grandparents and their grandchildren to spend quality time together sharing structured activities. Try involving grandparents in a storytime that they can attend with their autistic grandchild, or provide opportunities and guidance so that grandparents can read successfully with their autistic grandchildren. One program which taught grandparents strategies they could use outside of the library was created by the AutismBC Lending Library in Richmond, Canada. Called "Reading with Your Grandchild on the Spectrum," the program series consisted of six weekly sessions. During the sessions, grandparents were taught about autism and introduced to best practices in literacy and storytelling. The pilot program was funded through an "Autism Welcome Here" grant. If you want to do something similar but don't feel equipped to teach the sessions yourself, reach out to the autism-related organizations in your community. Through them you will most likely be able to find a facilitator who has the required availability and expertise.

Programs and Services for All Family Members

Parents, caregivers, siblings, grandparents, and other extended family members can all gather together and find value in more general autism-related programming and services offered at your library. The following ideas should appeal to these family members and also to other users of your library, including those with no connection to autism at all. To make sure that everyone knows they are welcome, try to promote these services widely and be sure to use language in your promotional materials that doesn't imply the program is exclusively for their autistic family members.

Host an "Ally" Program

Invite members of the community, as well as the family members of autistic people, to a program about being an autism ally. A successful program might include a panel of self-advocates or a single speaker, a discussion of chapter 9 ("Allies") from ASAN's open-access book *Welcome to the Autistic Community*, and an invitation for attendees to sign the "Pledge for Autistic Inclusion" which accompanies that chapter.[8]

MAKE IT VIRTUAL
Ask your community members to join you online for an "ally" program and sign the pledge as you're logged in together.

Host an After-Hours Event

Librarian Jen Taggart holds an accessible "ArtABILITY" event after the library is closed, allowing patrons with disabilities and their families to explore art and activities in a less crowded, low-stress, sensory-friendly environment.[9] The library is filled with artwork on display from the local school district, and various other activities are set up throughout the building. Librarians provide a visual guide to the event in the lobby, along with handouts and information about which art pieces are "touchable." An ASL interpreter attends, and librarians provide guided tours, sensory activities, and tactile art activities using materials such as fabric and pipe-cleaners. A cool-down space is available for anyone seeking a sensory break.

Host an Autism Acceptance Book Club

You can host an autism acceptance book club, or provide access to an existing or library-created virtual club. Ask teen and adult family members and other interested people from the community to read the same book on their own. Then provide space for them to convene and discuss the book, either in your meeting room or online. You can facilitate the discussion as you would in any other book discussion program, or provide the meeting

MAKE IT VIRTUAL
Ask your community members to view an online book club program on their own, and then gather together later virtually to discuss the book and session with one another.

space and ask a member of the local autism community to facilitate the group. Librarian Adriana White provides a good list of titles by age group later in this chapter that you can start with, and for advanced readers, you should try Steve Silberman's book *NeuroTribes*.

You should also consider providing access to an existing virtual book club for teens and family members. To do this, the planning and implementation of the program would be essentially the same as for a program led by an on-site facilitator, but you would also need to have technology available so you and your participants can log into the online chat as a group. Try setting up a big screen or a projector with a webcam, so all attendees can easily see the screen and be seen by the facilitator. One such program that we recommend is called "That Au-Some Book Club," which you can search for on Facebook. This is a Facebook

Autism Moms

In the autism community, using the term "autism mom" is sometimes seen as a negative. Autistics argue that this term, when used to describe a parent in relation to their child, is too close to describing someone as something like a "soccer mom." They feel it does not accurately represent autistic children or the parent's relationship to their autistic child. After all, autism is more complex than playing soccer!*

*Kaylene George, "We Need to Chat about Being an Autism Mom," Autistic Mama, https://autisticmama.com/shouldnt-use-autism-mom-identity.

book club that was started by a parent who calls herself "Not an Autism Mom." As stated in their welcome message, the group reads and discusses books as recommended by the autism community, and every other book has at least one autistic author. The moderator regularly conducts live sessions featuring the authors, and participants can ask these authors questions online in real time.

Host an Advocacy Series

Librarian Becky Fesler at the NorthWest Library in Oklahoma City arranged a series of four programs covering the varying stages of life that autistic individuals or their families may face. Fesler placed special emphasis on supporting individuals across the age span, and inviting speakers who are actually autistic themselves. As she says:

MAKE IT VIRTUAL
You can provide advocacy sessions live online and allow time for participants to ask questions and engage with one another at the end. You can also record the sessions for those who want to view them at a later time, and make them available on your website, with the presenters' permission.

> From my experience, getting special education services for children gets harder and harder the older they get. Diagnosis and early intervention [are] important, but we also need to stress that children do not grow out of autism. Teenagers and adults with autism need assistance and understanding as well. Teenagers in general, and especially those on the spectrum, need to learn how important it is for them to self-advocate. Three of the four speakers for the presentation on 'Autism in the Workplace' were autistic. I try very hard to seek insight and representation from people with autism, along with professionals in the field.

Fesler established three goals for the series:

1. Provide the community with valuable information related to autism at no charge in a welcoming environment.
2. Provide autistic individuals and their families an opportunity to meet other individuals facing similar life circumstances.
3. Increase awareness of the needs of autistic individuals among the community as a whole.

You can easily replicate Fesler's program at your library, using the following program plan.

ADVOCACY SERIES

NorthWest Library, Oklahoma City, Oklahoma
Developed by librarian Becky Fesler

What You'll Need

Local community experts and advocates

Program Series Description (Provided by Becky Fesler)

"The specific impact of being on the autism spectrum can vary from family to family. But wherever you and your family find yourself, both on the spectrum as well as your phase of life, you can find resources and tools in one of our four unique sessions designed to help navigate the ins and outs of the challenges and impact of autism in your life. Each session focuses on helpful tools for the stage of life you are in: early childhood and diagnosis, navigating resources for your school-aged child, the teenage years, and adulthood and workplace challenges."

Session One: Autism Identification and Advocacy for Young Children

In this session, we will discuss ways to have your child assessed to see if they are in need of special education services or need assistance through one of the other federal laws governing persons with disabilities. We will also discuss the importance of parents being advocates for their children.

Session Two: Autism Advocacy: The Teenage Years

This presentation will address autism advocacy issues. Parents and professionals play an important role in the life of a young child regardless of the disability. As children grow, they question their abilities and challenges. It is our responsibility, as parents and professionals, to teach the necessary skills to young adults as they engage in the transition process. Self-advocacy can be useful in many different ways, and in many different situations. It is important to draw on self-advocacy skills whenever it is important for the individual's voice to be heard. This includes situations in which medical/care plans are being reviewed or put in place, during assessments, and whenever an individual feels that they are being treated unfairly. Self-advocacy is an essential skill for all individuals, but in particular those who are on the autism spectrum.

Session Three: Autism Advocacy: Adults and the Workplace

In this session, we will discuss best practices and the challenges that adults on the autism spectrum face in the workplace.

Session Four: IEP and 504 Information

In this session, we will be discussing basic rights in special education, as well as individualized education programs (IEPs) and 504s.

Host Sensory-Friendly Movies

Sensory-friendly movies are more common than ever at local theaters, and this is a program many libraries are also finding success with. There are a few simple ways you can ensure your movie programs are more inclusive. Leave room in the back for children to pace or stim, and let participants know they are welcome to move around, dance, sing, and make noise. Keep fidgets available as children sit and watch or walk in the room, and offer ear plugs, headphones, sunglasses, and other sensory tools. Have LEGOs or coloring sheets available for kids who need to do something else during the film. Keep the lights only slightly dimmed, and lower the volume. Try to control the room for other sensory distractions such as sights, smells, and sounds. Librarian Renee Grassi hosts sensory-friendly movie programs, and she says it is important to make an announcement at the beginning to simply "come as you are" throughout the show.

Create a Resource Center

The entire family, as well as the professionals who work with them and the community at large, can be served by an autism resource center such as the one at the Lancaster (PA) Public Library. Established in 2010 with funds from an LSTA grant, the center has print, audio, and video collections on the subject of autism, computers with Boardmaker software, and other relevant materials. Along with providing materials and resources for information and support, the center also serves as a comfortable learning environment for autistic children themselves. The Lancaster Public Library has offered other related programs, including classes on the use of the Boardmaker software.

The Bloomfield Township (MI) Public Library's "accessibility support collection" includes toys, discovery skills kits, speech and language cards, story boxes, books, magazines, ASL story kits, and DVDs and CDs that support and represent disability experiences. This collection was developed by librarian Jen Taggart through collaboration with special education teachers and therapists in the district, and has been in operation since 2009. Another example is the autism resource center at the Oceanside (CA) Public Library funded through an "Autism Welcome Here" grant. The collection includes books, therapeutic toys, assistive technology, and speech and language card sets.

If you are not able to create a full resource center, there are still ways to incorporate some of these practices into your library. Does your library have a makerspace? If so, you may be able to request software such as Boardmaker to be purchased and installed within that space. In your children's section, you can load Zac Browser onto the computers. Zac Browser is a free internet browser you can easily download that has been designed specifically for children on the autism spectrum.

Representing Autistic People and Their Needs in Collections

Over the past decade or so, libraries have tried to ensure that autistic people and families can find related materials by creating special autism or disability collections. While this can make browsing easier, the concept is problematic. Imagine shelving all of your materials, both fiction and nonfiction, about Jews or people of color in one collection. If that idea horrifies you, then the idea of doing that with books about autism should as well. If you have such a collection and it is valued by your community, then keep it. If not, we suggest that you reshelve these books and consider how you can designate these materials in your catalog so that they are easy for patrons to find in a search. You can also create a booklist that highlights quality titles about autism, special education, disability law, and other related topics. We list some titles below that belong in every library for you to consider buying if you don't already have them, and more suggestions for building your collection are in "Appendix C: Building Your Collection." If you purchase these or other new books, consider mentioning them in e-mails that you send to your families to alert them to upcoming autism-related or inclusive programs they may want to attend. This gives you another excuse to reach out to families while promoting your programs, and another way to develop your relationships with this segment of the community.

MAKE IT VIRTUAL
You can add not just to your physical collection, but to your virtual collection as well. Make sure you keep your e-book collection updated with quality autism titles that can be accessed beyond the library's walls.

AUTISTIC AUTHORS
Adriana White

As a child, I was a voracious reader. I was also awkward and had trouble making friends. Through reading, I learned social norms and conversation skills. When I entered my teen years, I had a lot of questions about who I was, and what my purpose was in life. Books provided insight and ideas.

While research on autistic identity is a relatively new field, we do know that exposure to autistic culture improves the mental health and identity development of autistic children and teens.

One of the best ways we can help autistic kids is to provide them with positive models of autistic culture and identity. Books with autistic characters, written by autistic authors, can have a great impact on readers.

Some examples of books that libraries can provide are the following ones:

- Picture books by autistic authors
  - » *Flap Your Hands* by Steve Asbell, illustrated by Steve Asbell [Spring 2021]

> » *The Obsessive Joy of Autism* by Julia Bascom
> » *Too Sticky! Sensory Issues with Autism* by Jen Malia, illustrated by Joanne Lew-Vriethoff
> » *Benji, the Bad Day, and Me* by Sally J. Pla, illustrated by Ken Min

- Middle-grade books by autistic authors
  > » *The Half-Life of Planets* by Emily Franklin and Brendan Halpin
  > » *Get a Grip, Vivy Cohen!* by Sarah Kapit
  > » *The Many Mysteries of the Finkel Family* by Sarah Kapit [Spring 2021]
  > » *The Someday Birds* by Sally J. Pla
  > » *Stanley Will Probably Be Fine* by Sally J. Pla, illustrated by Steve Wolfhard
  > » *Me and Sam-Sam Handle the Apocalypse* by Susan Vaught
  > » *Can You See Me?* by Rebecca Westcott and Libby Scott

- Young adult books by autistic authors
  > » *Underdogs* by Chris Bonnello
  > » *On the Edge of Gone* by Corinne Duyvis
  > » *Please Don't Hug Me* by Kay Kerr
  > » *Rogue* by Lyn Miller-Lachmann
  > » *The State of Grace* by Rachael Lucas
  > » *Queens of Geek* by Jen Wilde
  > » *The Place Inside the Storm* by Bradley W. Wright

- Nonfiction books by autistic authors
  > » *The Spectrum Girl's Survival Guide: How to Grow Up Awesome and Autistic* by Siena Castellon
  > » *Nerdy, Shy, and Socially Inappropriate: A User Guide to an Asperger Life* by Cynthia Kim
  > » *A Freshman Survival Guide for College Students with Autism Spectrum Disorders* by Haley Moss
  > » *Middle School: The Stuff Nobody Tells You About* by Haley Moss

As a middle school librarian, here are three books that I was very excited to add to my collection:

1. *Get a Grip, Vivy Cohen!* by Sarah Kapit
   Kapit is autistic herself, and has voiced her disappointment at the way that autistic characters are usually portrayed—as emotionless adults who don't understand love or burdensome siblings.

2. *The Someday Birds* by Sally J. Pla
   Pla and her son are both autistic, and she thinks books with autistic characters can help both autistic and neurotypical readers to be more accepting and understanding.

3. *Me and Sam-Sam Handle the Apocalypse* by Susan Vaught
Vaught, a neuropsychologist, wants to see more books with autistic and disabled characters, so more kids can see someone like themselves doing amazing things.

There are also authors who have not written explicitly about autism, but are still writing great books. Tom Angleberger (*The Strange Case of Origami Yoda*) and Mike Jung (*The Boys in the Back Row*) speak openly about their autism on social media. In nonfiction, several autistic authors have written autobiographies and memoirs, including John Elder Robison, Temple Grandin, Michael McCreary, Laura James, Michelle Vines, Dawn Prince-Hughes, and Anand Prahlad.

While some neurotypical writers have been able to re-create the autistic experience, we should always prioritize stories by autistic writers. As evidenced by the popularity of the #ownvoices hashtag (created by autistic author Corinne Duyvis), our readers want to hear these authentic stories.

It is also important to support the voices of autistic writers with intersectional identities. First developed by Kimberlé Crenshaw, the idea behind intersectionality is that a person will face unique challenges in life, based on the combination of their race, gender, class, sexuality, and other factors. People of color and queer authors with autism have their own unique stories to tell that should also be heard. When we listen to stories from multiple diverse voices, we develop a greater understanding of autism and neurodiversity.

Stories teach kids empathy, help them relate to others who are not like them, and help them to see the value of a diverse world. Neurotypical kids who read books about neurodiverse characters can gain empathy and respect for autistic people. They may also learn how to make the world a more autism-friendly place, and join autistic teens in changing the world.

Because parents and other adult family members will value nonfiction informational texts about autism, and these books may be prohibitively expensive for them to buy on their own, make sure to have at least some of these works in your library's collection. You might also consider purchasing works of fiction that have autistic family members as characters. You may have to start small, but even a few of these books on hand at the library will be greatly appreciated by families with autistic members.

To get started, consider adding the following respected informational works:

All the Weight of Our Dreams: On Living Racialized Autism (2017), edited by
Lydia X. Z. Brown, E. Ashkenazy, and Morenike Giwa Onaiwu*
The Reason I Jump: The Inner Voice of a Thirteen-Year-Old Boy with Autism
(2016), by Naoki Higashida*
Uniquely Human: A Different Way of Seeing Autism (2015), by Barry Prizant
NeuroTribes (2015), by Steve Silberman

denotes autistic authors

New titles are constantly coming out in print. Be sure to constantly evaluate and update your autism collection just as you already do with your library's general materials. Appendix C lists places you can find updated autism-related booklists, as well as a number of publishers that specialize in material about autism. Check out their catalogs or websites to find recent works you can add to your collection. It is important to look at these sources because much of this material is not reviewed in the regular library media that you may use for collection development.

Though public and school libraries typically are not able to subscribe to individual research journals, you might refer parents with an interest in scientific studies about autism to their local academic library. Academic journals of interest include *Autism, Journal of Autism and Developmental Disorders (JADD), Focus on Autism and Other Developmental Disabilities, Autism Research,* and *Research in Autism Spectrum Disorders (RASD)*. Academic libraries often offer free services for community members, or the option to purchase an access pass.

MAKE IT VIRTUAL Some libraries have curated robust digital collections or LibGuides for their patrons interested in autism—this is a great way that anyone can access resources online. Take a look at some examples of them in Appendix C, which were developed by autism and disability self-advocates and librarians. Though many LibGuides are created for academic libraries, the information in them is still highly applicable to all library patrons with an interest in autism. You can incorporate these digital collections into your physical space by saving them as home screens on your computer stations. Depending on your situation, you might replicate something similar for your patrons, or simply direct them to collections that are already available.

ON YOUR COLLECTION: PROPOSING THE "2015 RULE"   *"Justin Spectrum"*

I propose that the year 2015 represents a turning point in the conversation about autism, rendering older resources on the subject to be obsolete. Any informational book on autism, whether for a young or parent audience, should be weeded if it was published before 2015. Any fiction book for kids or teens should be scrutinized through a "disability studies lens" with questions as to how it represents Autistic people.

Why 2015? Perhaps first and foremost, the aforementioned *NeuroTribes* was published in 2015 and won the former Samuel Johnson Prize as the outstanding nonfiction book of that year written in the English language. Upon receiving this award, Silberman described *NeuroTribes*' story as "the long journey of a group of people toward freedom and self-determination" and "the great story of our time."[10] *NeuroTribes* helped to push the concept of neurodiversity into the mainstream conversation and to position Autistic rights as civil rights.

Second, 2015 also marked the birth of #ownvoices, with a tweet on September 6 by the autistic author Corinne Duyvis to "recommend kidlit about diverse characters written by authors from that same diverse group."[11]

Third, while the *DSM-5* took effect in 2013 and eliminated "Asperger's syndrome" as a diagnosis, in 2015 many were still stubbornly clinging to the construct. Pre-2015 books would be far more likely to reference the Asperger's or "high functioning" construct that is continuing to fall out of favor, especially with self-advocates. By 2022 (with the release of the ICD-11) the diagnosis will no longer exist outside of the U.S. either.

Fourth, it is quite likely that your library owns books that talk about autism in a highly problematic and plainly inaccurate way. Some are quite obvious, such as Jenny McCarthy's books that have (among other things) promoted chelation therapy as a treatment for autism. Chelation therapy is not evidence-based and likely is dangerous.[12]

The "2015 Rule" is a starting point; post-2015, there have continued to be harmful books related to autism released by major publishers. *To Siri with Love* by Judith Newman is an example of why #ownvoices matters, and why "autism parent" memoirs should be examined skeptically. The book was released in August 2016 to positive reviews. In late 2017, self-advocates began to discover the book's harmful content, and wrote about it extensively online. Among the criticisms were that the author openly advocated sterilizing her own son, that she revealed potentially embarrassing tidbits about her son Gus without his consent, and that in a more general sense she maligned the Autistic community.[13] *To Siri with Love* raises broader questions: Who should tell the stories of autistic people? Why are autism parent narratives directing the conversation about autism?

Our understanding of autism continues to transform at a rapid speed. Narratives centering Autistic people and using a "disability studies" lens to view autism are nascent. Books that are older than five years old are most likely out of date in their discussion of autism.

"Nothing about us, without us." Those five words should be on your mind when making decisions about your collection. Autism parent narratives so often center the journey of the non-Autistic narrator. While public libraries of course need to consider popular demand, as Autistics continue to find their voice, the popular demand for Autistic-centered books will only rise!

Final Thoughts

Welcoming all family members through inclusive programming and a library-wide culture of inclusion is the best way to provide truly meaningful services for autistic children and teens, as well as the people who love them. But some programs that specifically address the needs of families with an autistic member are often useful as well, and we have introduced both approaches in this chapter. Some of the suggestions and examples in this chapter may take more time and funding than it's possible for all libraries to manage, and some ideas may need to be adjusted to best fit your community. However, all librarians can replicate or modify at least some of the practices we propose to start building a more inclusive environment that serves everyone in the family and the community. Start small and build on your successes over time. We're sure that your community will appreciate the efforts you make, and can help guide you to each new step on the journey to full inclusion.

NOTES

1. Not an Autism Mom, "Autism Didn't Ruin That Event. My Own Expectations Did," May 29, 2019, https://notanautismmom.com/2019/05/29/events-one.

2. Autistic Self Advocacy Network (ASAN), Welcome to the Autistic Community (Autistic Press, 2020), https://autismacceptance.com/book/a-note-for-families.

3. Kaiser Permanente, "Autism Risk in Younger Children Increases if They Have Older Sibling with Disorder," *ScienceDaily*, August 5, 2016, www.sciencedaily.com/releases/2016/08/160805230101.htm.

4. Dee Phair, "Unpacking the Diagnostic Tardis," in *All the Weight of Our Dreams: On Living Racialized Autism*, ed. Lydia X. Z. Brown, E. Ashkenazy, and Morenike Giwa Onaiwu (DragonBee, 2017).

5. Carol M. Singer, "Considering the Needs of Siblings of Individuals with Asperger Profiles," Asperger/Autism Network (AANE), www.aane.org/considering-needs-siblings-individuals-asperger-profiles.

6. Sesame Street and Autism, "The Sibling Experience," Sesame Workshop, 2015, https://autism.sesamestreet.org/wp-content/uploads/2015/08/SiblingGuide.pdf.

7. Jennifer L. Hillman, Michele C. Wentzel, and Connie M. Anderson, "Grandparents' Experience of Autism Spectrum Disorder: Identifying Primary Themes and Needs," *Journal of Autism and Developmental Disorders* 47, no. 10 (2017): 2957–68.

8. Autistic Self Advocacy Network (ASAN), *Welcome to the Autistic Community*.

9. Jen Taggart, "ArtABILITY: Accessible After-Hours Discovery at the Library," May 22, 2019, *Adaptive Umbrella*, https://adaptiveumbrella.blogspot.com/2019/05/artability-after-hours-accessibility-at.html.

10. Michael Roddy, "American Steve Silberman's *NeuroTribes* Wins British Book Prize," Reuters, November 2, 2015, www.reuters.com/article/us-books-samueljohnson/american-steve-silbermans-neurotribes-wins-british-book-prize-idUSKCN0SR2FB20151103.

11. Corinne Duyvis [corinneduyvis], "#ownvoices, to recommend kidlit about diverse characters written by authors from that same diverse group," September 6, 2015, Twitter, https://twitter.com/corinneduyvis/status/640584099208503296.

12. Emily Willingham, "No Evidence Supporting Chelation as Autism Treatment," *Forbes*, November 30, 2012, www.forbes.com/sites/emilywillingham/2012/11/30/no-evidence-supporting-chelation-as-autism-treatment.

13. Kaelan Rhywiol, "Why I Believe *To Siri with Love* by Judith Newman Is a Book That Does Incredible Damage to the Autistic Community," Bustle, December 8, 2017, www.bustle.com/p/why-i-believe-to-siri-with-love-by-judith-newman-is-a-book-that-does-incredible-damage-to-the-autistic-community-6780420.

Programming in School Libraries

SCHOOL LIBRARIES ARE IDEAL PLACES FOR AUTISTIC STUDENTS TO begin a lifetime love of books and libraries. School librarians have the benefit of working with every student in the school and seeing those students on a regular basis. They also have access to other professionals who work with these students, so they are better able than their public library counterparts to learn what their autistic students need and to customize their programs accordingly. Even so, many school librarians feel unprepared to directly support autistic students. If you are one of those, by the time you finish reading this chapter we hope you will feel more comfortable planning programs and lessons, and feel excited to begin better meeting your autistic students' needs.

School Library Scenarios

School librarians work with autistic students who attend school in a variety of settings. Here are the most likely scenarios you might encounter:

- Your school may have a dedicated autism program, where every child in the room is autistic, or you may work for a school that serves only autistic students. It may be easier for librarians in these situations to plan and implement programs specifically for autistic students than it is for librarians who must deal with different student groupings, some of which include autistic students.
- You might work with a special education self-contained class that includes, but is not limited to, autistic students. This model is typically used for those students with more serious disabilities who need the most support. You'll have access to the students' IEPs, which can help you learn who would benefit from targeted autism supports. Though not all students in these classes will be autistic, if you apply some of the best

practices we cover in this book, the programs you design are likely to be enjoyed and appreciated by the non-autistic students as well.

- Your school might practice full integration or inclusion. In this scenario, all autistic students are taught alongside their neurotypical peers in general education classrooms. In this case, you will also have access to IEPs, so it will be easy for you to ascertain which students have an autism diagnosis. As with the other scenarios, you should consider getting to know each of the included autistic students, working to meet their individual needs, and applying some of the ideas we have presented throughout this book in our discussions of inclusive programming.
- Finally, regardless of which class model you work with, it is highly likely that you will have undiagnosed autistic students in both self-contained and inclusive classrooms. You will not have IEPs for these students, so integrating inclusive practices into all of your library programs will ensure you are meeting the needs of all of your students.

What Is an IEP?

IEP stands for "individualized education program." Every student with a disability must legally have this plan, which is specifically developed by a team of professionals to support that individual's educational needs. The IEP team typically consists of a member of the special education staff (who often serves as team leader), the parents, and one or more autism-knowledgeable staff members, such as a speech and language, physical, or occupational therapist. Sometimes outside consultants or even lawyers are brought into the IEP meetings at the request of the parents. School librarians are not usually a part of this team, but they do have access to the plan created annually for each student.

As you read through this chapter, think about your own school environment and how you can tailor our suggestions and approaches to best fit the situation in your school.

INCLUDING STUDENTS ON THE AUTISM SPECTRUM
Sarah Brandow

Integrating students on the autism spectrum into a mixed-ability group takes some extra planning and forethought, but it is very worthwhile and rewarding. Mixed-ability groups can be positive for all students involved for many reasons. The experience all students get spending time with people who are different can help them learn to be comfortable with and not fear those differences. There are several practical ways to improve the library space and lessons to make everyone more comfortable and help everyone succeed.

One important thing to consider is the space. Having the entire class sit on the carpet for storytime may not work well for students with physical disabilities or attention difficulties. Students who are uncomfortable sitting on the floor may be more likely to disrupt those around them, and having only one student sit in a chair singles them out. Research has shown that dynamic seating can help. Gaming-style chairs that rock, bungee chairs, and beanbag chairs are all good options. It's good to have a variety so that students can choose what will work well for them. Paying attention to where you seat students is also helpful. Some students will focus better if they are in the front where they can hear and see better. Students on the autism spectrum might have trouble paying attention to a teacher in the front of the class, but if they are near the front, they are more likely to be engaged and less likely to be visually distracted.[1]

When planning activities consider all students. Make sure that there is are components that all students can complete. If students are filling in the blanks on something, give them printed answers that they can glue in place as an option. Assign student helpers to assist with activities that will likely be difficult. There are many ways that students on the autism spectrum with intellectual disabilities can be included in any activity.

It takes a little thought and planning to make sure that all students feel welcome and included in the library. Keep in mind that every student is different, and investing time to get to know students and try different things to see what works for them is important to ensure equity.

Three Things to Find Out about Each Student

If you know that a student you work with is autistic, it will make your work easier if you learn a few things about them. Dr. Mark Greenstein, a pediatric psychiatrist who worked with autistic children for many years, told Barbara in an interview that there are three questions any professional should ask:

1. What are this person's social needs?
2. What is this person's communication style?
3. Does this person have special interests?

If the child has a diagnosis, school librarians should be able to get the answers to these questions from the student's classroom teachers and therapists. Bear in mind as you work with these children that the emphasis is less on defining deficits and limitations than on looking at the individual's strengths and needs. This is what is done in the IEP process, and it is also a good guideline to follow in preparing for library programming.

Some things to consider as you address those three questions:

- Does this student prefer one-on-one attention, or can they participate well in a group?
- What motivates this student? This can revolve around a special interest.
- Does this student need time away from everyone else to process information?

What Is Echolalia?

In the behavior known as "echolalia," autistic individuals repeat words or phrases that they have heard or read. "Immediate echolalia" occurs when a person repeats words or phrases that someone else has just spoken. This can be used as a stalling technique while the child translates their thoughts into spoken language. It may also be used as a way to interact, or as a form of expression to make their needs and wants known. Think about what the child is trying to convey to you through those words. Perhaps the child is confirming something or agreeing with you by restating your words.

Delayed echolalia occurs when a person repeats a word or phrase seemingly out of nowhere, hours or days after they have heard or read it. This may be used to communicate, it may be part of sticking to a social script, or it may be a way to make needs known. Sometimes a child who uses delayed echolalia can fool you into thinking they have a higher level of comprehension and verbal skill than they actually do. Amythest Schaber covers these points in depth in their *Ask an Autistic* series, in "Episode #18: What Is Echolalia?" (www.youtube.com/watch?v=ome-95iHtBO).

- Are they speaking or nonspeaking? If speaking, do they display echolalia (repeats others' words or sentences) when they speak?
- What methods does the student use to communicate?
- Is the student more comfortable with written than with verbal communication?
- Does the student prefer to communicate with keyboarding (using a tablet or other electronic device)?
- Is it a good or bad idea to choose stories based on this student's special interest? Will they participate more, or will they get obsessively fixated?
- If the student is allowed to hold a favorite object during library time, will they be more likely to focus and participate?

Preparing Students for the Library Visit

Once you feel that you have a good understanding of the autistic students in your school, you are well on your way to developing appropriate programs for them. But before you bring the students into the library, refer back to chapter 3 for more detail on the following best practices in programming for autistic people. Apply them to your own programs whenever possible:

1. Limit enrollment.
2. Have teen or adult assistants.
3. Prepare participants for the program.

A Key to Success: Stimming

The child's behavior may give you a clue about their sensory needs. If they are stimming when they enter the library (i.e., doing self-stimulating activities like hand-flapping or rocking), it may be an indication that they are upset or that their vestibular system is seeking motion. A child should never be punished for stimming, but if it appears to be interfering with the quality of their library experience, you might provide an outlet for the child to self-regulate (like allowing them to walk around the room several times before sitting for storytime, or giving them a fidget object). If the child's stimming is not causing any problems for the group, let it continue—it may be just what they need to stay calm.

Programming in School Libraries

4. Use visual supports.
5. Manage transitions.
6. Control the environment.
7. Provide designated seating, with options.
8. Supply fidgets and other sensory tools.
9. Create quiet or sensory areas.
10. Incorporate repetition and routine.
11. Provide structure while being flexible and understanding.

Get to Know the Students' Paras

In a school environment, many autistic students will be assigned a paraprofessional aide, who accompanies and supports them throughout the school day and helps them to achieve their educational goals. This person can offer support during library time and can also be a source of information about the autistic student they work with. In your school they may be known by a different name, such as aide, ed tech, teacher's assistant, or educational assistant.

Some of these best practices will be more achievable than others in your library and school. Incorporate the ideas that you can, prioritizing those that will make the most difference for the students you work with. One way to ascertain which practices will be most impactful is to query classroom teachers, the student aides, and any other support staff who work regularly with the autistic students. You can also request that these professionals help prepare autistic students for library visits beforehand. It is also a great idea to ask the special education professionals for help developing a "Social Story" about what will happen in the library. Classroom teachers can share this story with their students prior to library time, or it can be sent home or posted on the school's website so parents can review it with their children on days that include library visits. In addition to the best practices, we cover other elements of successful programming in some detail in chapter 3, so be sure to review that entire chapter before proceeding to develop your lesson plans and programs.

EMPOWERING STUDENTS IN THE SCHOOL LIBRARY

Jessica Lyszyk

The American Association of School Librarians (AASL) encourages librarians to "demonstrat[e] an understanding of and commitment to inclusiveness and respect for diversity in the learning community."[2] Lauren Whitlock is a speech language pathologist who primarily works with students on the autism spectrum, especially those with extensive behavioral and communication needs and intellectual disabilities. She encourages librarians to consider ways to adapt library policies "so that they are explained clearly or can be tracked differently. For example, with due dates, it may be helpful for the students to see the date on an actual calendar that they can take with them and be able to count down days until it needs to be returned." Librarians should provide these accommodations, while considering ways to make students on the autism spectrum part of the library community. Whitlock encourages librarians to "consider the numerous vocational opportunities a library presents. Providing lessons or instructions on checking out books, shelving books, delivering late notices or materials to teachers, maintaining neat and clean spaces . . . are all skills and experiences benefiting students with autism." Empowering these students within the library space encourages inclusivity and builds student confidence.

Incorporate Instructional Strategies in Lesson Plans

School librarians can learn about and incorporate various instructional techniques to ensure that library programs help autistic students acquire knowledge and develop skills. Two educational concepts that are especially useful to consider, and that are often adopted by those in special education, are chunking and scaffolding.

Chunking is pretty much what the word sounds like: breaking lessons down into small, manageable segments. To understand scaffolding, think of a ladder. Before a child can climb higher, you have to determine which rung they are already on. To facilitate learning, it helps if each new lesson is based on what the person already knows and the skills they have already acquired. For this reason, it is useful to try to determine what your students already know before developing lessons or programs for them.

These concepts will be especially useful to consider when you conduct programs based on the regular educational curriculum. One way you might use scaffolding is by relating new concepts as you introduce them to the student's strengths or areas of special knowledge.

Create Connections

When planning library programming, try connecting it with the seasons, and with school or widely known community events. Talk to the teachers you work with, learn more about what they're doing in the classroom, and try to mirror or supplement that content. Think about what AASL standards the students are expected to meet and what library skills they need, and try to match those with what the class is studying and what is happening in the school. All of these connections can reinforce what classroom teachers are doing, and students will appreciate the familiarity of some of the content you introduce in the library.

Collaborate

You should reach out to the members of a student's IEP team, teachers or therapists who work well with the student, and the student's para as you plan individual supports. Not only can these team members help prepare students for a trip to the library, but they can also help you come up with program ideas that would work well in your library. These professionals may even have written resources that can guide you as you plan programs. Katie Kier, a librarian at the L. Douglas Wilder Middle School in Richmond, Virginia, says that collaboration with her school's "room parents," or parent volunteers, is helpful. Also, don't overlook collaboration with your local public librarians. Some public libraries have collections of professional materials that are a treasure trove of ideas, or they can let you know what works for them when your students attend the public library for programs. You can also collaborate with the other school librarians in your district. Many districts already have some way for these librarians to meet and work together on a regular basis. If your district has such a group, consider asking that at least one meeting a year be devoting to programming for your autistic students and others with IEPs. If it doesn't, think about creating one.

Provide Adapted Books

If you have the time and the resources, you can create "adapted books" for your autistic students. As librarian Heather Baucum says: "If you've never seen an adapted book before, it's because they come from one amazing source: your own hard work. Locating books on the correct reading level, pulling them apart, creating adapted words with reading supports, laminating, and putting it all back together is no easy feat. But a book that is structured to give a student on the spectrum their own reading independence is one of the greatest gifts that you can give them." These visual supports help students follow along while reading books, either together during a storytime or on their own. You might start by adapting books that you use regularly in your storytimes, then expand on that to provide an entire collection of adapted books for students to check out or use in the library. Or you can consider working with the other school librarians in your district to create these books. If you all create a couple and share them, you can easily have access to an entire collection to use throughout the year with your students.

Incorporate Routine

If you have classrooms that have library time on a regular schedule, you'll already have a head start in working with your autistic students, since they tend to appreciate structure and routine. In general, the library can be a safe, stable environment for these students, and you can make it even more so if you build repetition into what you do. Your autistic students won't be bored by repeated elements or even repeated books. Instead, they will likely find comfort in the predictability of the repetition.

Classes that visit the library probably visit other school "specials" as well, which can be stressful for autistic students, since the visits may present many new sensory experiences and new people to adjust to. You can counter this stress by finding ways to provide stability in the library. Some things you can do are: choose to read the same book at the start of every program, read the same book every day of the first week of school every year, or start each session in the same way and end it the same way for each visit. In inclusive classes, see which of these approaches your students respond the best to. The beginning-of-the-year routines can help students with their transition back to school after the summer.

Educate Your Community

We talked about how librarians are in a unique position to touch every member of the school community, so if you design thematic programs for the whole school, why not create programming based on autism, neurodiversity, and inclusion? Consider offering additional programs or devoting bulletin boards or displays to this topic throughout the school year. Baucum shows the video *Amazing Things Happen* to all of her kindergarten and first- and second-grade classes (www

MAKE IT VIRTUAL
Educational opportunities can easily go online if your library offers virtual programming. Students with access can stream the video from home, then join together in a virtual meeting room for discussion.

.amazingthingshappen.tv). She finds that this exercise helps her students build empathy for their neurodivergent peers as they talk about their own biases and neurological differences. As she puts it, "autistic kids live in a world that refuses to adapt to them. So every day they have to go through these patterns that don't make sense to them, and it's exhausting. We can meet them where they're at. That's the most beautiful part of humanity: that we can take care of each other. It's about compassion."

Programs across the Age Span

Remember that there are autistic people in every age group, and school librarians at every level will likely work with these members of the student body. As you read through this book, take note of the strategies that best apply to the age range you serve. If you work with elementary school students, you might find that the strategies and programs in our storytime and early childhood chapters can easily be adapted to your classes. If you work with middle or high school students, our "Programming for Teens" chapter may be helpful. We want to impress upon you that autism is not a childhood disorder, but one that is part of a person for their entire life.

The rest of this chapter is devoted to specific program ideas you can bring to your school library. It is by no means a comprehensive list, but it is intended to be a sampling of ideas you can replicate and use to jump-start your own planning process. We don't designate specific grade levels because the developmental level of your students may vary based on your classroom situation. However, we have grouped programs into elementary, middle, and high school categories. You will have to make your own judgment about which programs are best suited to the students you work with.

AN EXTRAORDINARY LIBRARY FOR UNIQUE STUDENTS
Amber Langston

In Nashville, Tennessee, one seasoned librarian is working within her school to provide library services to an extremely diverse group of students. Rebecca Ownby is in her seventeenth year as a librarian and currently holds the title of library media specialist at Harris-Hillman School in the Metro Nashville Public Schools division. The school is unique, as it is a public school serving students with disabilities from ages 3 through 21. Mrs. Ownby's main goal is to allow library materials and services to be accessible to each student enrolled at Harris-Hillman, while also preparing each student for the future.

The youngest group of students at Harris-Hillman School are those in the pre-K program, which includes children who are diagnosed with autism or with a speech delay. The storytime area that Ownby set up has modified seating consisting of cube chairs and stools. When the life skills classes come in for storytime, manipulatives in the form of tactile objects are used, along with button switches that she sets out for students to activate with their hands, feet, or any other part of their body. These switches have prerecorded sound effects that correlate with the story being read, and are ways for the pre-K students to engage with storytime regardless of cognitive or mobility status.

The oldest group of students that the library serves are those in the school's Community-Based Transition Program. Students in this program have graduated with a diploma from another high school in the area, but are welcomed back as Harris-Hillman students to receive further academic services and job training until they are twenty-one. During their time in the library this group works on activities to enhance their gross motor skills, as well as practicing social skills. Mrs. Ownby's primary focus when working with these students is to prepare them for life after high school. One approach she uses is to set up a self-checkout station in the library. This allows them to transition towards being independent users of the library, which she hopes will carry over into other aspects and roles that her students will take on out in the community.

From pre-K to age 21, Mrs. Ownby and the Harris-Hillman library serve a vast variety of students. To support each individual student and the classes as a whole, lessons are modified and individualized, additional support is granted, and understanding is addressed.

Elementary School: General Keys to Success

- Designate areas on the floor for each child to sit. Use cushions, mats, special seating like BackJack chairs, or colored tape.
- Use paper plates or baskets to hold craft supplies for each student, and label them with the contents.
- Use a puppet or squeeze toy as a turn-taking object. Tell the students they can speak when they are holding the object.
- If the students have trouble sitting still for the lesson, build in a short sensory integration break. Do a few jumps and stretches in place, or ask the students to stand facing the wall and pretend to hold it up by pushing with their hands. Or encourage activity and create a physical environment that allows for movement throughout the lesson. Be flexible.

Engagement

Don't mistake what you perceive to be a lack of focus as a lack of engagement. Baucum describes how one child she works with kicks the table while Baucum sings. At first glance, it may appear that the child is not listening. In reality, Baucum realized that she kicks in rhythm to the song—this is the child's method of engaging. You might also try tying a TheraBand around the chair legs for a student like this, giving them something to kick at that provides sensory feedback.

New Experiences

Try to expose your students to new experiences during library visits. Baucum uses Google Expeditions, which allows students to travel to new places virtually. She also has great success with "snowball" fights, using golf balls covered in soft foam. Any foam ball can work for this activity.

Motor Skills

Incorporate activities and practices that help to build motor skills. Studies indicate that autistic individuals can have varying degrees of difficulty with both gross motor skills (related to large muscle groups and affecting balance and general body awareness) and fine motor skills (using small muscles in the hands for precise movements). The "snowball" fights help students work on their gross motor skills. Library programs can also support fine motor skills. Once Baucum learned that working on fine motor skills was part of a student's IEP, she built lessons with that in mind. She made the connection that the motion used in the fingerplay for "Baby Shark" is the same one a child would use to pull up their coat zipper, so she incorporated that song and movement into lessons.

Supplies

You should always have a variety of supplies on hand to ensure students have ready options for learning and creating. You never know when inspiration will strike—either for you as the librarian, or for your students. Librarian Katie Kier suggests keeping the following in stock:

- Paper plates
- Glue sticks
- Craft sticks
- Jumbo crayons
- Construction paper
- Yarn
- Magnets

- Ziploc baggies
- Foam art brushes
- Single hole punch
- Pre-cut foam shapes
- Plastic silverware
- Dot art markers
- Googly eyes

- Dollar Store trinkets
- Pom-poms
- Jingle bells
- Cotton balls
- Coffee filters
- Chenille sticks (aka pipe cleaners)

Using Inclusive Practices in All Classrooms

Many programs that you're already doing with regular education classes can be enjoyed by your autistic students. Now that you have new knowledge about autism, think of ways to adapt these ongoing programs to make them more accessible and enriching, or develop new ones that your students can enjoy and learn from. For example, Baucum used a Makey invention kit to create an interactive digital zoo with her third-graders. Through this program, the students were able to feed their animals and give them water. While this was a program designed for all of the students in that grade, it was well-received by her autistic students. She found similar success when teaching her sixth-graders how to make an augmented reality game. These are two high-tech examples, but the lesson translates no matter what materials you work with. Take note of programs or lessons you offer that might have particular appeal to your autistic students, and find ways to make them more inclusive. You should also consider some new programs, such as the following three inclusive programs for elementary school students.

FROSTY THE SNOWMAN

Colonial Trail Elementary School, Glen Allen, Virginia
Designed by librarian Rachel LeClair

What You'll Need
- Silver or white glitter
- Clear Ziploc baggies
- Shaving cream, or Cool Whip for children who tend to put materials in their mouths
- 2 black plastic circles per student, about 1 inch wide
- 1 orange plastic triangle per student, about 1 inch wide
- 1 black plastic hat per student, about 1 inch wide

SAMPLE PROGRAM PLAN

While this inclusive program will be fun for all students, it is particularly great for those who are working on fine motor skills.

1. First, read or watch your favorite version of the Frosty the Snowman story. LeClair reads *Frosty the Snowman* by Steve Nelson.

2. Then, create baggie snowmen by inserting glitter, shaving cream, and plastic shapes to fill each baggie. Be careful not to fill the baggies too full, so they don't explode.

3. Students will have a great time making Frosty's face by moving the shapes into place to make eyes out of the plastic circles, a nose out of the plastic triangle, and the hat on top. You can also ask them to just find and identify each shape.

FIGURE 8.1
Frosty the Snowman Activity
Frosty the Snowman activity at the Colonial Trail Elementary School

POETRY BAG

Wilder Middle School, Richmond, Virginia
Designed by librarian Katie Kier

Ages: This program works best with older children

What You'll Need
- An opaque bag or container
- Small items such as an old key, bottle cap, sugar packet, comb, and so on.
- An eye cover such as a sleep mask
- Paper
- Markers

SAMPLE PROGRAM PLAN

1. First, put one small item at a time into your bag or container. Kier uses a small paper bag, but anything that is not transparent will work.

2. Invite a student to come to the front of the class and put on the eye cover. Students who are uncomfortable with the eye cover can simply close their eyes. Invite the student to put his hand in the bag and feel the object.

3. Then ask about five questions of the student, such as: Is it smooth or rough? Is it bigger than a quarter? Try to avoid too many open-ended questions. Write down the child's answers. At the end, ask them what they think the object is, and write that down too.

4. Finally, read the answers out loud or invite the student to read them to the class—you'll discover that the answers make up a poem about the object. Kier says that this program ends up being a lot of fun. It could easily be used in any type of classroom environment, although some autistic students may need prompting or assistance in order to participate.

STORYTIME WITH FELT BOARD OR ADAPTED BOOKS

Crossfield Elementary School, Fairfax County, Virginia
Designed by librarian Heather Baucum

Frequency: A half hour once a week

What You'll Need

Adapted books or a felt board and prepared felt pieces. You can buy felt by the yard and staple it to a foam board to create a simple and cost-effective felt board.

SAMPLE PROGRAM PLAN

1. Always start with greeting the kids. Talk about something related to the book, and pass out the visual support storyboards, adapted books, or felt board pieces.

2. If you're using adapted books, give each student their own board. The librarian or aide should have one to use as an example and will model placing pieces onto the book when you get to a certain point in the story.

3. If you're using a felt board, make sure each child gets at least one or two felt pieces. This will help everyone develop listening skills and give the children something to focus on—when you get to a certain point in the story, you can ask, "who has the (xyz) piece?"

4. Invite the child who has that particular felt piece to bring it up to the felt board and place it themselves. If they need help, they can hand it to the librarian, who can place it for them.

5. After reading the story, it is time to check out books. Model how to select a book and bring it to the desk for checkout, then let students go pick out their own books. Let them scan the books for checkout, with assistance if needed, so they feel ownership in the process.

Both the felt board and the adapted storyboards/books make for enjoyable fidgets, because kids enjoy feeling the textured pieces. Felt is an affordable material and is easily replaced if a child gets overly excited and damages a piece, which allows everyone to be in the moment and simply enjoy the experience. If you are able to laminate the pieces you use with your adapted storyboards, this is also a nice fidget for your kids. They are also easily replaced once the crinkle is gone or if a piece gets torn while being enjoyed. One tip that Baucum offers for both felt and adapted book pieces is to not skimp on color printing. The world runs in color, and for autistic kids who process information very literally, this more accurate representation helps them to make a connection between the story and real life and helps them move from the abstract to the concrete.

Middle and High School: General Keys to Success

In general, tweens and teens want to fit in with their peers. You should use inclusive practices whenever possible so an autistic student does not feel "othered." Some examples of these practices are:

- Have seating options available for all students (refer back to chapter 2 for more detail).
- Build consistency and routine into all library instruction.
- Avoid labels such as "special," "sensory-friendly," or even "autism" when designing and promoting events to support your autistic students. These students don't want to feel singled out in front of their peers. Instead, reach out to them directly to ask if they would like to participate in what you've planned, and let them know that you designed the program with them in mind.
- Do a signage audit. Are your policies posted, and is the messaging consistent and in simple, clear language? Are your visuals uncluttered? Does signage let students know where they can find a quiet space, and where they can be loud? Will a student who is a literal thinker be able to easily understand your messaging? Be sure you're not overwhelming students with visuals that are unnecessary or contradictory.

ACCESSIBLE TO ALL?
AN INSIDER'S PERSPECTIVE   *Jessica Kompelien*

Though the library can feel like a refuge for a majority of students, there are definitely some physical and emotional barriers the library presents to users with autism spectrum disorder. In Erin Phillips's words, "I can imagine it would be the last place they'd want to spend time."

Phillips, an author and high-school library assistant, is autistic, and she has many important points to note regarding the current state of her library and how it may be perceived by students who are on the spectrum. From Phillips's perspective, there are a few things that the library can do to make the space more comfortable for students on the spectrum. Her first idea was to provide ear plugs. These would be an inexpensive and disposable way for students to block out some of the noise of the environment. She also said that the library could purchase noise-canceling headphones. While expensive, these could be a great way for students to choose to lessen the sound around them as they listen to their own music, which could also be a source of comfort. Finally, Phillips brought up the idea of study carrels, which she noted "have fallen out of vogue in high school libraries" despite being a mainstay in college libraries. Not only do these spaces block out some of the environmental noise, but they also help eliminate visual distractions. Because her library is a huge, open room full of collaborative work spaces, these more isolated structures could help eliminate those visual distractions. As librarians, we cannot make assumptions about how our users will best learn and use our spaces; it is critical that we provide a variety of options, collaborative and individual, for all students to take advantage of so that they will feel more comfortable and welcomed into our spaces.

Lawrence wrote that "librarians generally agree that they should work directly with users to determine their information needs. Applying this thinking to Autistics is really just a reasonable extension of current practice."[3] This is the driving statement behind the philosophy of librarian Melissa Techman, who stresses how important it is to try to connect "with students to see what they like and what they need" by collecting user feedback. Techman has also found it incredibly helpful to watch ever-changing IEPs and 504s while communicating with classroom teachers about their students.

The library provides a unique opportunity for reflection on how best to serve neurodivergent students. Shea and Derry write that "patience and encouragement goes a long way when helping students with ASD."[4] These attitudes, when coupled with the practical solutions of mindful space design, tools to help eliminate distractions, and collaboration with classroom teachers, can truly make a difference in the way the library is perceived and used by students on the autism spectrum.

Try some of the following program ideas with your middle and high school students. You can modify the programs so they meet the needs of the students you serve.

Lunch Groups

With funding from an "Autism Welcome Here" grant, the Evelyn Hanshaw Middle School Library in Modesto, California, started an inclusive club for students called the Team Titans Club. Meeting in the library during the lunch break once every other week, students who attend are put in teams made up of both autistic and neurotypical students. The teams work together to play games and build puzzles, earning scores for their efforts. The scores are posted on a large monitor in the library, and the teams compete over time to see which one is the winner, earning books for everyone in the group. All participants are also given a Team Titan nylon book bag. The program was designed by school librarian Sherry Chapman and special education teacher Rachel Knoepfle, who wanted to provide the autistic students with an opportunity to socialize and build new peer relationships. Many students who came appreciated being able to spend their lunch period in the library, especially those who wanted to avoid the bustling and sensory-rich lunchroom. But this program did more than allow them to just eat their lunch in the library. It also gave them something fun to do and a chance to get to know their fellow students.

LUNCHTIME SANCTUARY

Janet Coulson

I work in a middle-school library and see firsthand how it offers a supportive social and emotional space for many students in our school community. I was first approached by our guidance counselors to assist students during their lunch period because many students have sensory issues and are simply overwhelmed when sitting in a noisy lunchroom with 500 peers. One of the guidance counselors came to me recently and asked if I could host three boys in the library during lunch. The counselor offers a supportive lunch-bunch twice a week, but one boy, despite attending her lunches regularly, was still seriously isolated. She wanted to brainstorm a way to engage this boy socially. Together we came up with a plan to have him and two other boys from his class come to the library during their lunch period to eat and play board games. After a few weeks, he began sitting with the other two boys and they now talk, laugh, and play games. Other students have approached me directly, asking if they may eat in the library.

We also have two students with physical disabilities who use wheelchairs, one of whom has an assistive technology device that helps her to communicate, who began eating in the library a few months ago with a staff member. Soon after, a few general education students began to join them each day, one of whom is on the autism spectrum. This arrangement has fostered socializing that would not be possible in the busy lunchroom. The result is the creation of a socially inclusive environment.

By offering a safe social/emotional space, the library undoubtedly benefits students academically as well. A lunchtime sanctuary gives students a place to calm and center themselves so they may reenter the classroom ready to learn. In addition, inclusive environments provide lessons in equity for all students by providing an opportunity for general education students to see students who need more support integrated into the daily fabric of the library; the environments also provide opportunities for them to interact and engage in a positive fashion. Creating inclusive services and environments benefits all students.

Transition Planning

The transition from high school to life after high school is a major life event for any teen. Unfortunately, this transition can present different and more serious stressors for autistic teens since their postsecondary options are often fewer. They are at high risk of having no employment or postsecondary education to move on to when compared to their peers, particularly in the first two years after high school.[5] You can help bridge this gap by developing inclusive programs and services to support older autistic students as they prepare for this major transition. One way to prepare older autistic teens for postsecondary education is to provide programming that lets them know what to expect in an academic library. You can bring in an academic librarian to present to the students. You can show video tours of a number of college and university libraries. You can work with your school guidance counselors to identify schools that offer good autism supports, and be sure to feature some of those in your virtual tours. Though some aspects of the library might be different in the institution your students decide to attend, most are likely to be similar to the libraries you introduce. Students who find comfort in their school library will be happy to know that a similar experience is available to them in college, and so they will be able to more easily negotiate the difference between their high school and college library environments.

Reference Help

Reference work is an essential library service, and knowing how to ask for reference help is an essential ingredient in student success. For autistic students, the skills involved in getting help will most likely need to be specifically taught. You can develop a program or record a webinar that teaches students how to use this service, as well as how to be most effective when they need to reach out to library staff for reference help. Describe the idea of the reference interview to them. Explain that the librarian is there to help and that the student is not bothering them by asking for assistance. Try to help students to conceptualize their information needs so the librarian will be best able to assist them. Teach students how to construct search terms when they do their

MAKE IT VIRTUAL
Virtual reference offers another option for autistic students who might do better working in a quiet environment of their choice away from school, or who want to work independently. If you introduce this service, be sure to include a clear link to your virtual reference service on your library's web page, and have this docked as the home screen on computer workstations.

own research, so they maximize their chances of getting useful results. All students will benefit from learning these skills, and autistic students will appreciate learning the rules of the reference experience.

SOCIAL CONSIDERATIONS   *Jessica Kompelien*

In addition to the environmental barriers that students with autism spectrum disorder might encounter, there are social issues to consider. Erin Phillips says that "social anxiety and fear of asking questions can also be an issue that autistic people struggle with, so asking [the library staff] for help finding a book or resource might be intimidating." Librarians must be aware of how their actions and reactions might be perceived by all patrons, especially those with ASD. Regardless of how friendly, patient, and accepting the library staff might be, a student with ASD might still have a great deal of fear when it comes to the social interaction necessary to find out information. "Unlike students who tend to reach out to librarians at their own volition, students with ASD can be more shy and insecure in asking for assistance."[6] This obviously poses a unique problem for these students and causes an inequity of access that ought to be considered. One suggestion to solve this problem comes from Remy and Seaman: "Chat reference is another avenue of online help that could benefit the ASD student who may not be as adept at face-to-face contact with a librarian."[7] In order to make inquiries more accessible for students with social anxiety, the library could set up a chat feature on the website that would allow students to approach the librarians in a more comfortable way.

A Final Note

Every school librarian who is interested in providing autism-focused programming must start somewhere. Try keeping a journal of reflections as you develop your practice, noting your successes and areas for improvement. And don't forget that any effort you're putting in place now is more than what was available to your students and school community before—so give yourself a pat on the back for progress achieved, and keep moving forward.

NOTES

1. High-Functioning Autism," Reading Rockets, 2019, www.readingrockets .org/article/teacher-s-brief-guide-teaching-students-high-functioning-autism.

2. American Association of School Librarians, *National School Library Standards for Learners, School Librarians, and School Libraries* (Chicago: American Library Association, 2018), 48.

3. Emily Lawrence, "Loud Hands in the Library: Neurodiversity in LIS Theory & Practice," *Progressive Librarian* 41 (2013): 105.

4. Gerard Shea and Sebastian Derry, "How Do We Help? Academic Libraries and Students with Autism Spectrum Disorder," *Recasting the Narrative* (2019): 353.

5. Paul T. Shattuck et al., "Postsecondary Education and Employment among Youth with an Autism Spectrum Disorder," *Pediatrics* 129, no. 6 (2012): 1042–49.

6. James Cho, "Building Bridges: Librarians and Autism Spectrum Disorder," *Reference Services Review* 46, no. 3 (2018): 330.

7. Charlie Remy and Priscilla Seaman, "Evolving from Disability to Diversity: How to Better Serve High-Functioning Autistic Students," *Reference & User Services Quarterly* 54, no. 1 (2014): 27

Training and Education

There are many places to turn to continue your education about autism. Consider the following websites and resources as a starting point.

TRAINING AND EDUCATION RESOURCES

Targeting Autism in Libraries

https://targetingautismlibs.com

This is a great place to start for training and education opportunities. View their "Resources" tab for resource lists, and their "Discussion List" tab to join the "Autism Works in Libraries" discussion group and continue the conversation.

Autism and Libraries: We're Connected

www.librariesandautism.org/index.htm

This is another excellent resource for training and education. View the "Use These Resources" tab to access downloadable resources you can customize for your library, and the "Watch This Video" tab to access a staff training video updated in 2014.

Project ENABLE (Expanding Non-Discriminatory Access by Librarians Everywhere)

https://projectenable.syr.edu/

Access free online autism and inclusion trainings for librarians and staff.

Project PALS (Panhandle Autism Library Services)

https://pals.cci.fsu.edu/

Access a free series of four online training modules about autism for librarians.

State Library of Illinois

www.cyberdriveillinois.com/departments/library/libraries/targeting-autism .html#Training

Access resources and view recorded webinars affiliated with the Targeting Autism initiatives.

Special Needs and Inclusive Library Services (SNAILS)

https://snailsgroup.blogspot.com/p/resources.html

SNAILS is a networking group of youth services librarians in Illinois providing services for youth with disabilities. They update an ongoing list of helpful resources.

TRENDS AND CONVERSATIONS

Bookmark the following organizations and websites to stay tuned in to trends and conversations, and learn from members of the autism community.

Autistic Self Advocacy Network (ASAN)

https://autisticadvocacy.org/

Wrong Planet

https://wrongplanet.net/

Amythest Schaber's "Ask an Autistic" YouTube channel

www.youtube.com/user/neurowonderful/

AUTISM-FOCUSED FACEBOOK GROUPS

- Autistic Allies Information Group
- Ask Me I'm Autistic
- Autistics in Libraries & Their Allies
- Neurodiversity Librarians

Recommended Resources for Intersectional Practice

Adriana White

Disability & Intersectionality Summit
www.disabilityintersectionalitysummit.com
Disability advocates Mia Mingus, Alice Wong, and Sandy Ho created the "Access is Love" project in 2019 to promote the idea that accessibility is not just a box to be checked, but an act of care and love. Libraries can use their "Actions to Take" and "Reading & Resources" pages on the Disability & Intersectionality Summit website as a foundation for creating more accessible library programs and spaces.

"How to Plan Events That Prioritize Accessibility"
www.thinkingautismguide.com/2019/10/how-to-plan-accessible-events.html
One resource of particular interest to librarians is the "How to Plan Events That Prioritize Accessibility" post by autistic advocate Lydia X. Z. Brown, which can be found on The Thinking Person's Guide to Autism website. Brown's recommendations include captions, scent-free environments, name tags, microphones, limiting flash photography, and more.

Twitter
There are many intersectional autistic hashtags on Twitter. By regularly reading through these hashtags, we can keep up with the concerns and celebrations of our diverse communities. These hashtags include:

#AutisticBIPOC	#AutisticWhileBrown
#AutisticPOC	#AutisticBlackJoy
#AutisticBAME (UK)	#SoyAutista (for Spanish-speakers)
#AutisticWhileBlack	#Autismo (for Spanish-speakers)
#AutisticBlackPride	#Neurodiversidad (for Spanish-speakers)

Following these hashtags on Twitter may leave you with a lot of questions. You can use the #AskingAutistics hashtag to ask a question, and the responses you get will come from autistic people. However, it is critical that we do not put too much work on the shoulders of BIPOC autistics. We need to do our research and due diligence. We need to read what has already been done without overwhelming the people who are already working hard to create change. And, most importantly, we should not further burden those who are already operating under great levels of stress and oppression. While libraries are encouraged to seek out diverse autistic professionals for input, every effort should be made to compensate them for this important work.

Project READY

https://ready.web.unc.edu
Librarians can study the Project READY curriculum, a free online professional development resource that focuses on "Reimagining Equity & Access for Diverse Youth." Project READY was created by librarians at the University of North Carolina at Chapel Hill, in partnership with the Wake County Public School System and North Carolina Central University. A diverse group of librarians, educators, and teenagers came together to develop a curriculum dedicated to equity and inclusion.

Building Your Collection

You can use the following tips and resources to build a collection of physical and digital materials on autism.

Autistic Self Advocacy Network (ASAN)

https://autisticadvocacy.org/resources/books

Turn first to the publications from ASAN, a collection of materials intended to benefit the autism community.

Ed Wiley Autism Acceptance Lending Library

https://neurodiversitylibrary.org/book-list

This library lends materials on autism "from a neurodiversity and disability rights & justice perspective," and their website provides an updated list of books they recommend.

Chicago Public Library

https://chipublib.bibliocommons.com/list/share/200049033/405410987

At the time of this book's printing, the Chicago Public Library had an updated list of books for children and teens. Try searching the site online for "autism recommended reads."

Libraries and Autism: We're Connected

www.thejointlibrary.org/autism/autismcollection.htm

This website was created by the Scotch Plains Public Library and the Fanwood Memorial Library in New Jersey. Among other things, the site lists the contents of the autism collection of these two libraries.

"Not an Autism Mom" Blog

https://notanautismmom.com/2020/07/20/autism-books

This blogger curated a list in 2020 of "100-ish" books on autism and neurodiversity. Included are her suggested Top 10 books to get you started, along with lists of books by autistic authors, books by non-speaking autistic authors, books for children and teens, and books for women.

Schneider Family Book Awards

www.ala.org/awardsgrants/schneider-family-book-award

These awards honor "an author or illustrator for a book that embodies an artistic expression of the disability experience for child and adolescent audiences."

LibGuides about Autism

- Massachusetts Library System: https://guides.masslibsystem.org/autism
- University of Illinois: https://guides.library.illinois.edu/autismspectrumdisorders
- University of Kentucky: http://libguides.uky.edu/autismresources

PUBLISHERS SPECIALIZING IN MATERIAL ABOUT AUTISM

AAPC Publishing

www.aapcpublishing.net

This publisher offers nontechnical materials about autism for parents and educators. Of particular interest is its support of the Super S.T.A.R. Storytime program created by Joanna Keating-Velasco at the Placentia Library.

Brookes Publishing

www.brookespublishing.com

This educational publishing company offers material on a range of topics, including autism. Its titles are research-based, and most of them are aimed at teachers and other professionals.

Future Horizons

www.fhautism.com

This company focuses exclusively on books and other materials about autism and related topics.

Jessica Kingsley Publishers

www.jkp.com

A British company with offices in the United States, Jessica Kingsley publishes a number of books on autism aimed at both professionals and parents.

Woodbine House

www.woodbinehouse.com

This publisher specializes in material about a variety of disabilities and related subjects for parents, professionals, and children.

Potential Funding Sources for Programs

The ideal situation is to have your autism-related programming covered by your library's regular budget. If that is not possible, consider approaching local parents' groups and foundations. If there are no local funding sources, you can consider applying for one or more of these grants:

ALA's List of Grants

www.ala.org/awardsgrants/awards/browse/grnt
Try searching ALA's comprehensive list of grants. View the current list on their website to see if any offerings align with your library's needs.

ALSC/Candlewick Press Light the Way Grant

www.ala.org/alsc/awardsgrants/profawards/candlewicklighttheway
This grant is for a library program serving an underserved population of children and is funded by the Candlewick Press in honor of author Kate DiCamillo.

Autism Welcome Here

http://librariesandautism.org/grant
Sponsored by "Libraries Autism: We're Connected" in honor of founder Meg Kolaya, this grant was created and is funded by Barbara Klipper. It is awarded annually to one or more libraries in the United States or Canada for programs or services that benefit autistic individuals or their families.

Dollar General Literacy Foundation

www.dgliteracy.org/grant-programs
This foundation offers youth literacy grants to public libraries and schools.

H. W. Wilson Library Staff Development Grant

www.ala.org/awardsgrants/awards/39/apply
This ALA grant is given to a library whose staff development is designed to further the goals of the organization.

Library Services and Technology Act (LSTA) Grants

Contact your state library for your LSTA grant application guidelines. There are LSTA grants specifically for programs that serve people with disabilities.

State Farm Good Neighbor Citizenship Company Grants

www.statefarm.com/about-us/community-involvement/community-grants/ good-neighbor-citizenship-grants

Educational institutions and programs conducted by government entities can apply for these grants.

Visualizing Libraries

https://libraries.foundationcenter.org

Another resource to use is Visualizing Libraries, a free tool developed by the Foundation Center to assist libraries in identifying grant opportunities of all kinds.

Resources for Program Support

VENDORS SELLING THERAPEUTIC EQUIPMENT

- Abilitations: www.schoolspecialty.com/abilitations
- Achievement Products for Special Needs: www.achievement-products.com
- Beyond Play: www.beyondplay.com
- Different Roads to Learning: www.difflearn.com
- eSpecial Needs: www.especialneeds.com
- Fun and Function: www.funandfunction.com
- Pocket Full of Therapy: www.pfot.com
- Therapy Shoppe: www.therapyshoppe.com

EDUCATIONAL AND TOY SUPPLY CATALOGS

- Constructive Playthings: www.constructiveplaythings.com
- Lakeshore: www.lakeshorelearning.com
- Oriental Trading: www.orientaltrading.com

WEBSITES FOR DEVELOPING STORYTIMES

- *Adaptive Umbrella* blog: https://adaptiveumbrella.blogspot.com
- Infiniteach: https://infiniteach.com/autism-resources
- Jbrary: https://jbrary.com
- Storytime Katie: https://storytimekatie.com

BOOKS ABOUT SENSORY INTEGRATION (SI) AND SI ACTIVITIES

Biel, Lindsey, and Nancy Peske. *Raising a Sensory Smart Child.* Penguin, 2018.

Foster, Stephanie M. *Self-Regulation and Mindfulness Activities for Sensory Processing Disorder.* Rockbridge, 2020.

Garland, Teresa. *Hands-on Activities for Children with Autism & Sensory Disorders.* PESI Publishing & Media, 2016.

McPhee, Mary. *Sensory Activities for Autism: Fun Learning Games for Autism and Sensory Disorders.* Edx Autism, 2019.

Sher, Barbara. *Everyday Games for Sensory Processing Disorder: 100 Playful Activities to Empower Children with Sensory Differences.* Althea, 2016.

Watts, Mandisa. *Exciting Sensory Bins for Curious Kids.* Page Street, 2020.

WEBSITES FOR SENSORY INTEGRATION ACTIVITIES

- Raising a Sensory Smart Child: www.sensorysmarts.com/sensory_diet _activities.html
- Sensory Processing Disorder (SPD) Resource Center: www.sensory -processing-disorder.com/sensory-integration-activities.html
- Your Kids Table: https://yourkidstable.com/sensory-diet-activities

Sensory Integration Activities

Adapted from lists originally prepared by Barbara Klipper
for the Ferguson Library, Stamford, Connecticut

BOOKS AND RELATED SENSORY ACTIVITIES

Just Like Daddy by Frank Asch

Use a magnetic fishing game to go fishing, or use attached chopsticks or tongs to go fishing, picking up Swedish Fish candies (easier) or goldfish crackers (hard).

Mr. Gumpy's Outing by John Burningham

Have the children lay on their stomachs on small carpet squares. Use arms and legs to raft around the room. Then lie on back and repeat.

From Head to Toe by Eric Carle

Do the movements from the book.

Mrs. Wishy-Washy's Farm by Joy Cowley and Elizabeth Fuller

Play with small plastic animals in chocolate pudding (finger painting, smelling, and tasting are just fine).

Freight Train by Donald Crews

Use a train whistle (or just go "toot, toot"). Have children push the Educubes around the room in a line like a train. You can also sing or play a train song while you do this.

Go Away, Big Green Monster! by Ed Emberley

Throw beanbags at a large picture of a green monster (on poster board or flannel board). Vary the distance or use color, number, alphabet, and/or weighted bean bags for variety and different challenges.

The Wide-Mouthed Frog by Keith Faulkner

Using a frog animal swing-lid can, toss dragonfly beanbags or plastic bugs into the frog's mouth. Extend the lesson by offering other foods to the frog and discussing who eats or doesn't eat them.

Roller Coaster by Marla Frazee

Line up Educubes like roller coaster cars. Give the children clacker fidgets and encourage them to make the sound of the roller-coaster going up the incline. Hold arms up and yell as they go "down." Then have them "get off," stand arm's length apart and spin around in one direction once, and then in the other direction. (Don't do the spinning with kids who have seizures, and stop if you see signs of overstimulation or discomfort.)

Split! Splat! by Amy Gibson

Put small plastic animals, people, and other toys in a large plastic bin. Give the children small spray bottles and let them "rain" on the objects. Ask them to put their hands in the spray to feel the water. Also make sun and tree props for each child using cutouts and craft sticks. Play Raffi's song "Mr. Sun" and act out the sun hiding behind the tree and the sun coming out.

Mary Had a Little Lamb by Sarah Josepha Hale

Use a lamb puppet as you read the story. Print out coloring pages of a lamb and have the children glue on cotton balls for the wool.

Jump, Frog, Jump! by Robert Kalan

Have the children start in a squat and do a frog jump or kangaroo jump. Practice jumping all together, then have individual kids jump when you call their name, say the color they are wearing, and so on.

Please, Baby, Please by Spike Lee and Tonya Lewis Lee

Have one or more sensory balls on the floor. Have the children sit on the floor in a circle. Take turns rolling the ball to different children and have them roll it back to you. You can sing the song (to "Row, row, row your boat") "Roll, roll, roll the ball, roll the ball to (insert child's name), (child's name four times), roll it back to me."

Pete the Cat: I Love My White Shoes by Eric Litwin

Use white Ellison die-cuts of sneakers. Let the children color them red or blue to go with the colors in the book. Also, have blueberries, strawberries (defrosted frozen works best), and water. Give the children small pieces of white fabric (from a cut-up handkerchief) to squish in the fruit. Rinse out the squares in water with a little lemon juice.

Here Are My Hands by Bill Martin, Jr., and John Archambault

Caregivers draw (or trace) body parts on carpet squares with sidewalk chalk. The children erase chalk marks using their body parts (hand, elbow, foot, etc.).

Un Elephante: Number – Numeros by Patty Rodriguez and Ariana Stein

Take three or four elephant stuffed animals. Set out a parachute and have the children stand around it holding on. Start with one elephant standing on the parachute and have the children shake the parachute to upset the elephant's balance. Keep adding elephants one at a time. Alternate activity: make a very simple spider web with tape on the floor. As you play the song, have the children walk around the web trying to stay on the tape lines. Search YouTube to stream and play the song "Un Elefante Se Balanceaba," a popular Spanish nursery rhyme, while you do the activity.

Pete's a Pizza by William Steig

Do some of the actions from the book (no tossing in the air). Use cardboard cutouts for pizza toppings. Have adults massage the children with deep pressure to roll out the dough. You can combine this with a pizza craft.

Build a Burrito: A Counting Book in English and Spanish by Denise Vega

Provide bath towels or yoga mats. Have caregivers roll the children up in the towels or mats like a burrito. Play a calming song while the children stay rolled up. If they want, caregivers can apply deep pressure to the children while they're rolled up.

Mouse Paint by Ellen Stoll Walsh

This activity involves edible color mixing. Use food coloring and Cool Whip. Pre-make bowls of red, blue, and yellow Cool Whip. Give the children empty ice cube trays and spoons to use to mix colors.

I Went Walking by Sue Williams

Walk on sensory stepping stones or other tactile items in bare feet or socks. You can use percussion to keep a beat, or ask the children to vary how they move from stone to stone (jump, hop, giant step, etc.).

RHYMES AND RELATED SENSORY ACTIVITIES

1, 2, 3, 4, 5, Once I Caught a Fish Alive

1, 2, 3, 4, 5,
Once I caught a fish alive.
6, 7, 8, 9, 10,
Then I let it go again.

Play a magnetic fishing game or pick up Swedish Fish candies or goldfish crackers using tongs or animal-topped joined chopsticks.

Blow, Wind, Blow

Blow, wind, blow!	*That the baker may take it,*
And go, mill, go!	*And into bread make it,*
That the miller may grind his corn;	*And bring us a loaf in the morn.*

Blow pinwheels (or turn with fingers). Touch the cornmeal. Knead the pre-made pizza dough (add a little flour to make it stiffer) or Play-Doh.

I'm a Little Teapot

I'm a little teapot, short and stout,
Here is my handle,
here is my spout.
When I get all steamed up
then I shout,
"Tip me over and pour me out!"

Act out the rhyme, but add rapid jumping or bouncing up and down (for boiling) at "steamed up." Pour cold water from a pot into a cup.

Jack and Jill

Jack and Jill went up the hill to fetch a pail of water,
Jack fell down and broke his crown,
And Jill came tumbling after.

Children can act as Jack and carry or lift sand pails filled with weighted beanbags. Children can also act as Jill and roll on the floor.

Jack Be Nimble

Jack be nimble,
Jack be quick,
Jack jump over the candlestick.

Children squat down and then jump up in place. The leader models jumping over a candlestick, rope, and so on. Don't jump from a standing position.

La Vaca Lola (with translation)

La vaca lola, la vaca lola	*Lola the cow, Lola the cow*
tiene cabeza y tiene cola.	*She has a head and has a tail*
La vaca lola, la vaca lola	*Lola the cow, Lola the cow*
tiene cabeza y tiene cola	*She has a head and has a tail*
y hace muu	*and says moo.*

Take a clothesline rope or woven jump rope and tell the children we're going to pretend it's a cow tail like Lola's tail. Lay the rope stretched out on the floor and have the children jump back and forth over it. See how many children can jump over it ten times. Have adults nearby to make sure kids don't trip on the rope. To make it more secure, tape the rope to the floor securely on both ends. Stream the "La Vaca Lola" song by El Reino Infantil on YouTube while the children play.

Little Boy Blue

Little Boy Blue,
come blow your horn.
The sheep's in the meadow,
The cow's in the corn.
Where is the boy that looks after the sheep?
"He's under the haycock, fast asleep."

Breathe-and-blow activities: blowing bubbles or paper blowouts. You can also have the children lie down and pretend to sleep as you cover them with a weighted object such as a heavy quilt. Or you can cover the children with a yoga mat or towel, and have the parents put weight or deep pressure on the children.

London Bridge

London Bridge is falling down, falling down, falling down.
London Bridge is falling down,
My fair lady.

Have two adults make the bridge by linking hands. Children go under the bridge by crawling, walking on knees, rolling, and so on.

Old King Cole

Old King Cole was a merry old soul,
And a merry old soul was he;
He called for his pipe,
And he called for his bowl,
And he called for his fiddlers three.

Blow bubbles with bubble pipes, or blow on paper party blowouts. You can also make this a counting activity, with flannel board figures of the fiddlers. Start with one figure and add one at a time until you have all three.

Pat-a-Cake

Pat-a-cake, pat-a-cake, baker's man,
Bake me a cake as fast as you can;
Pat it and prick it, and mark it with a B,
And put it in the oven for baby and me.

Use Play-Doh, or some other modeling substance. Have the children write letters or shapes in the substance, with their fingers if possible.

Pin Pon (with translation)

Pin pon es un muñeco	*Pin pon is a very handsome*
muy guapo y de carton	*cardboard doll*
se lava la carita con agua y con jabón.	*He washes his face with water and soap.*
Pin pon siempre se peina	*Pin pon always combs*
con peine de marfil	*with an ivory comb*
y aunque se hace tirones	*and even if he pulls hair*
no llora ni hace así.	*he does not cry.*
Pin pon dame la mano	*Pin pon give me your hand*
con un fuerte apretón	*with a strong squeeze*
yo quiero ser tu amigo	*I want to be your friend*
pin pon pin pon pin pon.	*pin pin pon pin pon.*

Pre-draw simple child shapes on paper and/or cardboard. Give each child a sheet and scissors (have adaptive ones on hand for those who need them). Have children cut out the Pin Pon shapes and decorate them with stickers or crayons. This is a fine motor activity; the cardboard will give more resistance. Search and stream the "Pin Pon" song on YouTube; we like the version by Toy Cantado.

Twinkle, Twinkle, Little Star

Twinkle, twinkle, little star,
How I wonder what you are.
Up above the world so high, like a diamond in the sky.
Twinkle, twinkle, little star,
How I wonder what you are.

Darken the room. Shine the flashlight beam on different objects in the room and identify the objects in the light. Also give each child a rubber band. Have the children pull them apart with thumb and pointer fingers side to side, and then up and down with each word.

Keys to a Successful Library Visit

Barbara Klipper
Adapted from a pamphlet for parents, produced by the
Ferguson Library, Stamford, Connecticut

THINGS TO DO AT HOME

- Find out if your local library has a Social Story describing a visit, or create your own. Read the Social Story with your child before you go, so they know what to expect.
- If your library offers tours, arrange to do one with your child before a visit to use services, get materials, or attend a program. If the regular tour will be too crowded or is not right for your child in other ways, contact your library to see if you can arrange a personal tour at a quiet time.
- Include library visit time in a daily schedule that you create for your child. Review the schedule with your child throughout the day. Help them anticipate the library visit as a fun thing.
- An activity that involves brushing, swinging, gum-chewing, heavy work like lifting or pushing objects, and/or wearing a weighted vest can help some autistic children manage stress and organize themselves. Consider using some or all of these tools before a library visit. Consult your occupational therapist before you use these tools for the first time.
- Time the library visit for success, when your child is not tired, hungry, or overloaded, and when the library is relatively quiet and empty.
- If your child is non-speaking, use AAC such as a picture communication system (PECS) so your child can communicate directly with the librarian and others.
- Find out the details about any library program you plan to attend so you can decide if it is developmentally appropriate for your child, and identify if any accommodations are needed.
- Before a program, find out if you will be expected to stay with your child and if you will be needed to assist the librarian during the program.

THINGS TO DO AT THE LIBRARY

- At a time when the library is quiet, introduce your child to the library staff, describing to them what is most likely to lead to a meltdown. Request any needed accommodations and discuss with the librarians how best to meet your child's needs.
- Facilitate transitions for your child. For example, give them a ten- and five-minute warning before their computer time is up. Bring a visual timer with you if that is a tool you use at home.
- Create and stick to routines during library visits, or prepare your child beforehand if you will have to deviate from the routine.
- Be on the alert for unusual noises or events that could upset your child, such as a running vacuum cleaner or a substitute librarian at a story-time program. Take your child aside to address these issues. Sometimes this can help your child feel safe and avoid a meltdown.
- Don't be embarrassed if your child is a little noisy or talks out of turn to the librarian. If you have introduced the child to the staff, they will be accepting of these behaviors.
- Find out if your library has a sensory room or other quiet place and bring your child there if they become dysregulated. When they are calm again, you can return to what you were doing at the library.
- If the library doesn't offer them, bring fidgets or noise-canceling head-phones for your child to use during programs and library visits.

About the Contributors

Sarah Brandow, Janet Coulson, Hope Hill Clark, Shannon Hoggatt, Karen Kinsey, Jessica Kompelien, Amber Langston, Jessica Lyszyk, and **Reina Malakoff** are MLIS students at Old Dominion University in Norfolk, Virginia.

Steph Diorio is an autistic archivist and local history librarian who plays *Splatoon* too much. When she's not playing at being a squid with a Super Soaker, she can be found writing and drawing comics, doing comedy history research, or spending time with her 22-pound cat, Murphy. You can follow her on Twitter @1863_project.

Tina Dolcetti's enthusiasm for literacy and excellence in early childhood education inspired her to become the children's librarian at the Moose Jaw Public Library. In 2020, Moose Jaw Public Library won the TD Summer Reading Club Accessibility Award based on the efforts of Dolcetti and her dedicated team.

Karen Stoll Farrell is the associate librarian for South and Southeast Asian studies, and head of the Area Studies Department at the Indiana University Libraries. She was the coeditor of *Heading East: Security, Trade, and Environment between India and Southeast Asia* (2016). She has published four entries in *Online around the World,* and coauthored a web archives piece for the *Journal of Western Archives.* Her service revolves around open access and digital humanities for South Asian and Southeast Asian materials. Her current research interests include early Indian film ephemera, services for Autistic patrons, and web archiving for Area Studies.

Charlie Remy has been a professional librarian for a decade and is on the autism spectrum. He is the electronic resources & serials librarian and an associate professor at the University of Tennessee at Chattanooga. His hobbies include speaking Spanish, lifelong learning, international travel, and, more recently, cooking. Charlie received his MS degree in library and information science from Simmons University and his BA from Elon University.

"Justin Spectrum" is the pseudonym of an Autistic children's librarian. He holds an MLS degree and is working toward an MA in disability studies. In preschool, it was observed that Justin was "full of questions and wants to know 'why' everything is so." This desire to know "why" eventually led Justin to receive an autism diagnosis as an adult. Justin enjoys the relational aspect of being a children's librarian, and helping young readers find the right book. He is interested in disability representation, especially in middle-grade books. You can follow Justin on Twitter @justinspectrum.

Kate Thompson is a reference librarian from Des Moines, Iowa. She is the proud spouse and parent of autistic individuals and thanks them for the learning opportunities they've given her. She received her MLIS degree (with a youth studies emphasis) from the University of Alabama, where she was the editor of the *Crimson Review of Children's & YA Literature*. She gives presentations to library employees on inclusive children's programming and accessible environmental design, and to physician groups as a disability advocate. Her writing has been featured in the digital edition of *American Libraries* and on ALA's *Intellectual Freedom Blog*.

Adriana White is an autistic school librarian in the South San Antonio Independent School District. Prior to this role, she worked as a special education teacher for five and a half years. She also leads professional development sessions focused on what teachers and librarians can learn from autistic adults. Adriana earned a master's degree in education, with a concentration in special education, from the University of Texas at San Antonio. She earned a second master's degree, in library and information science, from the University of North Texas, along with graduate academic certificates in storytelling and youth services in libraries.

Paul Wyss went to Indiana University in 1996 to work as the library liaison for Walden University. In 1997 Wyss began working as a distance learning librarian at the University of South Dakota. Wyss worked there until 2000, at which time he took a job as the web designer for the Oshkosh (WI) Public Library. He worked in Oshkosh for one year and then began working at the University of Wisconsin at Stout, in Menomonie. In 2004 he began a position as a distance learning librarian at Minnesota State University at Mankato. He was diagnosed with Asperger's syndrome in 2007.

Heidi Zuniga is a librarian and associate professor at Colorado State University. She previously worked at Ithaca College and the University of Colorado, Anschutz Medical Campus. She has an MA degree in English and an MS in library science. She spends most of her time outside of work with her family, but her other interests include running, listening to audiobooks, and learning more about autism.

Index

f denotes figures

CPSIA information can be obtained
at www.ICGtesting.com
Printed in the USA
LVHW051619131222
735145LV00009B/639